MacKay

A VISITOR'S GUIDE
TO THE
ANCIENT WORLD

Lesley Sims

Illustrated by Emma Dodd, Christyan Fox,
Ian Jackson, Ian McNee and John Woodcock

Additional illustrations by Inklink-Firenze
Designed by Ian McNee and Lucy Parris
Edited by Jane Chisholm

History consultant: Dr. Anne Millard

CONTENTS

**For Internet links see pages
178 and 198-199**

WHERE IN THE WORLD?

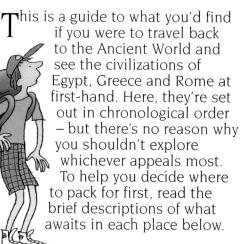

This is a guide to what you'd find if you were to travel back to the Ancient World and see the civilizations of Egypt, Greece and Rome at first-hand. Here, they're set out in chronological order – but there's no reason why you shouldn't explore whichever appeals most.

To help you decide where to pack for first, read the brief descriptions of what awaits in each place below.

ANCIENT EGYPT

You'll visit Egypt during the reign of Ramesses II, also known as Ramesses the Great – especially to himself. He was pharaoh, or king, of Egypt from about 1289 to 1224BC. (Don't be confused if you come across various spellings of his name elsewhere. Ramses and Rameses can also be used, but they're all the same king.)

EGYPT: PROS & CONS

Tourism in Egypt doesn't take off until the Greeks arrive in the 6th century BC. You'll see the country in its unspoiled glory, but you'll be fending for yourself. There are no hotels, no tour guides and no embassy if you hit trouble.

If you still want to visit, the best times to go are October or March, either side of the extreme summer heat. March has the added bonus of harvest festivals, on top of exploring the pyramids and mummy factories, and partying Egyptian-style.

A RIVER CRUISE

One of the best ways to see Egypt is from the river Nile. You can travel the length of the country from the Mediterranean to the edge of the Nubian desert. Ramesses II is currently building a new capital city for himself at **Per Ramesses**. It's a good starting point for a boat trip as many boats set off up the Nile from here.

The map below shows some suggested stop-off points on the cruise

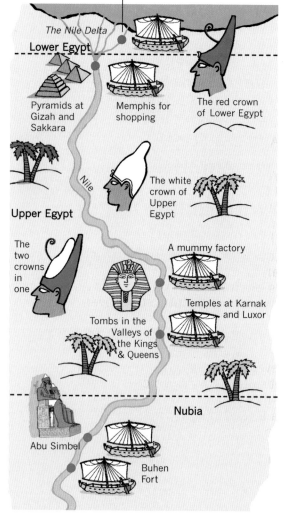

Ramesses' new capital, Per Ramesses, in the Nile Delta

The Nile Delta

Lower Egypt

Pyramids at Gizah and Sakkara

Memphis for shopping

The red crown of Lower Egypt

Nile

Upper Egypt

The white crown of Upper Egypt

The two crowns in one

Tombs in the Valleys of the Kings & Queens

A mummy factory

Temples at Karnak and Luxor

Abu Simbel

Nubia

Buhen Fort

ANCIENT GREECE

If you're looking for a break which mixes culture with the beach, head to Greece. The best period to visit is between the years 479 and 431BC, when the man in charge is Pericles (who'll dominate Athenian politics from 443-429BC). He's famed for his dignity, eloquence and, in an age of the back-hander, his incorruptibility.

Greece is a mountainous country in southern Europe bordered on three sides by the Mediterranean Sea.

GREECE IS THE WORD

Hitch a lift on the bandwagon to Athens

Trade is flourishing, cities are rich and, under Pericles, the city-state of **Athens** is at the forefront of an art explosion. Join the cream of dramatists, sculptors and philosophers flocking to Greece, and see for yourself what an inspirational country it is.

On the other hand, if sports are more your thing, this is your chance to see the original Olympics in the flesh (literally – competitors don't wear clothes).

ANCIENT ROME

Your final choice is **Rome** around 118AD when the Roman Empire is at its height. Emperors have been in charge for just over 100 years and the city's population has exploded to a million people plus (huge for an ancient city). The reign of Trajan is ending; Hadrian, the new man at the top, is about to take over.

It's a place of great contrasts, from wealth to grinding poverty and, like every modern city, it never stops. It's also hot, noisy, crowded and smelly. But, unlike Egypt, Rome is a tourist destination. There's plenty to do, for residents and visitors alike, from gladiator fights and chariot races to shopping and relaxing at the baths.

ROME: A FAST-MOVING CITY

Just one word of warning! Rome is constantly changing, with new buildings going up all the time. Some of the things you read about in here may well be different by the time you arrive.

Old buildings are torn down and new ones erected as each emperor puts his mark on the city.

5

USING THE GUIDE

Wherever you visit, you'll find all the information you need in this book. Separate sections cover where to stay and what to eat, suggestions for sightseeing and trips out of the main cities. As well as smaller, detailed maps, there are also three large maps to help you find your way around. Finally, historical background has been included for each civilization, with details on topics such as religion, education, government and fashion.

VISA INFORMATION

The good news is you won't need a visa – or passport – to visit Egypt, Greece or Rome. All three are fairly hospitable places welcoming foreign visitors. All that's required is respect for the country you're visiting and its people's way of life. Just remember if you visit Greece: after a month, resident "aliens" must register with the authorities and pay taxes.

Glance at this map of the Roman Empire and you'll see why foreign visitors – in Rome especially – don't raise an eyebrow. They make up a large proportion of the population.

The Empire reached its largest extent with Trajan's defeat of Dacia (present-day Romania).

WEATHER

All three destinations are warm, becoming insufferably hot at the height of summer, though Egypt is by far the hottest. Greece has rainy winters and Rome is prone to mild showers, even in the summer months.

In Egypt a fan is essential (though this one needs a servant to carry it).

Both Greece and Rome can be visited in late spring or early summer, though Egypt would be too hot. If you want to include a trip to **Olympia** in Greece for the Olympics (pages 98-99), the Games don't begin until the very end of June.

The Roman Empire in 117AD: the Romans control most of Europe and beyond

Occupied territories

Fortified walls to keep out enemies

BRITAIN GERMANY
Black Sea
GAUL DACIA
Atlantic Ocean
ITALY
ASIA
Corsica Rome
SPAIN Sardinia Aegean Cyprus
Sea
Mediterranean GREECE Crete
Sea
AFRICA

WHAT TO PACK

Since you'll be moving around, travel light. (For Egypt, all you really need are insect repellant and that fan.) But if you have a light tent and sleeping bag, it's not a bad idea to bring them with you. Camping is often a tourist's only option.

A water bottle is another useful item. You'll drink a lot in the heat and the usual canned drinks aren't available. There are no refrigerated drinks stands on hand either – just plenty of fountains, rivers or wells where you can fill up with fresh water. (There's little pollution, so the water is perfectly safe.)

WHAT TO WEAR

On arriving, make a market your first stop to buy the local dress. In Egypt think little and loose, though at least the heat is dry rather than humid. Generally, tunics and sandals are ideal for all three places, though in Rome, to blend in properly, you'll want to buy a toga. (See page 168 for tips on wearing it.) To protect against the sun and dusty paths in Greece, many people wear a broad brimmed hat, and riding cloak (called a *chlamys*).

DOS & DON'TS

The Ancient World tends to be a conventional place. So, to make the most of your stay, remember these hints. They won't only save you from social embarrassment – they could save you from arrest.

Cleanliness: To be sure of fitting in, you can't just be clean but super clean. The Egyptians in particular are fanatical about hygiene. In their hot, dusty climate, with sand which gets everywhere, they spend hours washing themselves and their clothes.

His 'n' hers: If you're visiting in a mixed group, you may have to split up. In Greece, for instance, men and women live in separate rooms at home and they lead pretty much separate lives. Men dominate all ancient societies, in public at least, and gender discrimination is a fact of life. Whether it's something you've grown up with or not, here you'll just have to get used to it.

Most women have sheltered existences – Greek wives in rich families rarely leave home at all. Although Egypt and Rome are more relaxed in this area, it can prove a minefield for the time tourist in Greece. So, in the section on Ancient Greece, any activities which are strictly all male are indicated by this symbol:

Males only

TOP TIPS & QUOTES

On many pages, you'll find extra hints for things to do and how to behave. You'll find them in boxes similar to the ones shown here. These have your first and probably most important tips for visiting Egypt, Greece and Rome.

TOP TIPS FOR TOURISTS (EGYPT)

No. 1: Ouch!

Be sure to check your shoes for scorpions before putting them on, or you could get a nasty shock. There are few snakes in Egypt, though be warned: those that do live there are extremely dangerous, so keep your distance.

TOP TIPS FOR TOURISTS (GREECE)

No. 1: Don't mention the war!

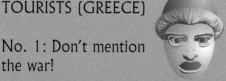

And don't mention the Persians. They invaded in 480BC, destroying the holiest temples in their excitement, and were only defeated a year later. If you visit soon after – 478BC say – you'll see it's (understandably) still a touchy subject.

TOP TIPS FOR TOURISTS (ROME)

No. 1: Citizenship

Whatever else you forget, REMEMBER THIS VITAL PHRASE: *"Civis Romanus sum"* (say *Key-wiss Row*, as in boat, *mar-nuss sum*). It means, "I am a Roman citizen".

Roman citizens have more rights than anyone else (see page 123). So even if the phrase can't get you out of trouble, it will certainly ensure that the trouble is less severe.

QUIRKY QUOTES

Many pages also have quotes, from visitors or famous locals. Quotes are shown like this:

> " *The quotes give useful insights but they are personal opinions and don't reflect the views of the writer of this guide...* "

ALL MAPPED OUT

Over the page is a fold-out map to Egypt, with various sights picked out to make your sightseeing easier. You'll find a map of Ancient Greece between pages 75 and 76, and a map of Ancient Rome between pages 141 and 142.

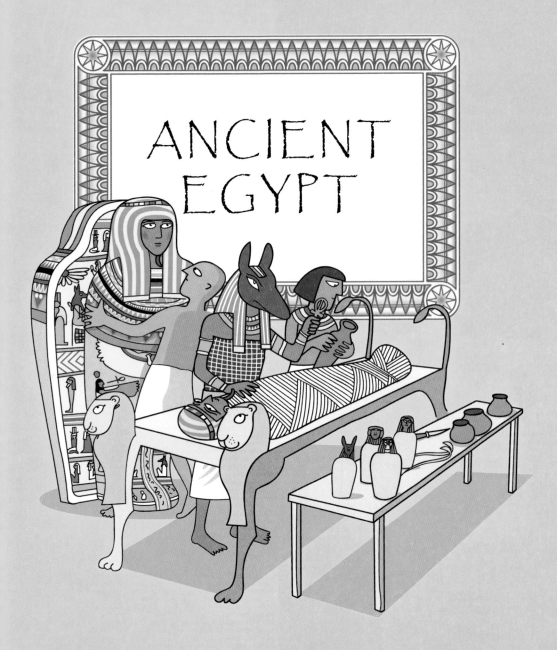

ANCIENT EGYPT

ANCIENT EGYPT: MAIN SIGHTS

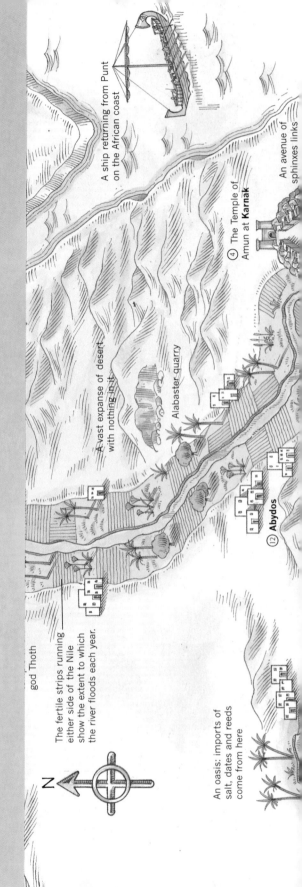

A ship returning from Punt on the African coast

An avenue of sphinxes links

④ The Temple of Amun at **Karnak**

A vast expanse of desert with nothing in it

Alabaster quarry

god Thoth

The fertile strips running either side of the Nile show the extent to which the river floods each year.

⑫ **Abydos**

An oasis: imports of salt, dates and reeds come from here

N

MAP OF ANCIENT EGYPT AND NUBIA

⑤ The Temple of **Luxor**

⑧ **Thebes** & mummy factories on the West Bank

Aswan (known as Syene)
A city on the Nubian border

Tomb of Queen Nefertari

Tutankhamun's funeral mask

Edfu

Elephantine Island

First Cataract

⑥ **Valley of the Kings**
⑦ **Valley of the Queens**

⑨ **Nubia**

A Nubian gold mine (where part of Egypt's wealth comes from)

An area between the First and Second Cataracts occupied by Egypt during the New Kingdom

⑪ Ramesses II's temple carved into the rock at **Abu Simbel**

Second Cataract

⑩ **Buhen Fort**, one of a ring of nine forts

ABOUT EGYPT

Originally, Egypt wasn't one but two kingdoms. Ramesses II's official title is still "King of Upper and Lower Egypt", though you're unlikely to get close enough to him to use it. The box below gives you all the history you'll need for your visit. If you're not interested in history, skip straight to the (far more important) practical stuff.

Ramesses II on his throne.

A BRIEF HISTORY

Egyptian civilization can be traced back to about 5000BC (Before Christ was born). For convenience, historians split Egyptian history into periods (see pages 192-193). Ramesses II ruled during one of the most important: the New Kingdom.

Originally, Egypt was a collection of villages along the banks of the Nile, the river which runs from north to south on the eastern side of North Africa. By 3200BC, the villages had united, forming two independent kingdoms. Called Upper and Lower Egypt, each fought to control the other.

A slate carving of an Upper Egyptian king executing a prince from Lower Egypt

Then, in about 3100BC, Menes, a king of Upper Egypt, conquered Lower Egypt, and united the kingdoms. Menes founded a capital at Memphis and his family became the first of 31 dynasties, or ruling families, to govern Egypt.

PRACTICALITIES

Bartering & bribes: A basic money system using copper weights is in place, but generally goods and services are simply bartered or exchanged. Even wages are paid in food. Take a plentiful supply of spices with you – they're a popular currency. You'll get an excellent rate of exchange for silk and pepper, as the Egyptians don't have either. Not only will you need goods to buy things, they also make useful presents. Although many places aren't officially open, guards will often show you around in return for a suitable "gift".

Insect repellant: This is vital but if you want something chemical, you'll have to bring it from home. More environmentally friendly is to follow the Egyptian example and use a leaf.

Measures: The main unit of measurement is a *cubit*, which is the distance from an adult's elbow to his or her fingertips. Because measurements vary depending on whose arm is used, there's also a *Royal Cubit* (52.5cm or 21in), which is standard across the country.

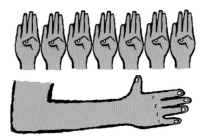

For smaller measurements, palms (of hands) or digits (fingers) are used. Seven spans or 28 digits make a cubit.

Weights: Egyptian weights are stones or pieces of metal, often shaped like animals. The basic weight is a *deben* which weighs about 91g (3.64oz). One deben is made up of ten *kites*; ten debens (100 kites) make a *sep*.

EMERGENCIES

Finally, if you do get into serious trouble, call the equivalent of the police: the *Medjay*. There are Medjay in all the major towns, keeping law and order, catching criminals and guarding the frontiers. Many of the Medjay are recruited from Nubia.

The Medjay use "sniffer" dogs to track down criminals.

HOW TIME FLIES

Information on time, the Egyptian calendar and the seasons can be found on page 64 but, in the box below, there's one handy time fact you may like to know upfront:

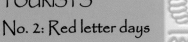

TOP TIPS FOR TOURISTS

No. 2: Red letter days

The Egyptian calendar is full of "good" and "bad" days marked in red (which were days when good or bad things had happened to their gods). Don't do anything at all on a bad day. It may end in disaster.

66 Would that I were in the country always... 99

Taken from an early manuscript

11

GETTING AROUND

Egypt's major highway isn't a road at all but a river, the Nile. With roads virtually non-existent, and wheeled vehicles few and far between, it's your best bet for getting from one place to another.

Most villages are near the Nile, and temples on the desert edge are connected to it by a network of canals. You'll find journeying by river is efficient and very reliable. (Which may be a change from getting around back home.)

BOATING

Because boats are the main way to travel, there's a wide choice, from ferries to cargo ships and grain barges. Ferrymen ply their trade between east and west banks, charging a couple of small copper weights at most.

CRUISING

For a longer trip up the Nile, jump on a boat heading south. The most luxurious are the royal barges. You're unlikely to hitch a ride on one of these, but you may be able to talk your way on to an official's state ship. Otherwise, don't expect the equivalent of a modern cruise ship. You'll be lucky if your boat has a canopy. You'll wash in the river and eat and sleep on the river bank – but you wouldn't want to be stuck in a stifling cabin. Besides, sitting on an open deck is the best way to see the countryside.

To tell if a boat is going south, look for a sail. The current flows downstream (north), while the prevailing wind blows upstream (south). So, boats heading south need sails, while those going north use oars.

South (sail up)

North (sail down)

Hieroglyphs (picture writing)

A busy scene on the Nile

From dawn until dusk, the river is crowded with every type of craft.

A barge transporting obelisks (square stone columns with pointed tops)

A noble's boat with decorated deckhouse

An oar is used to steer the boat.

> **When the Nile [floods] all of Egypt becomes a sea, and only the towns remain above water...**
> Herodotus, an Ancient Greek historian

LAND TRAVEL

Few roads exist, and those that do are all within towns. There's no point having roads link one town to another. The Nile floods once a year and they'd simply be washed away. Not only that, farmers need what little land there is for raising crops.

If you pictured yourself sweeping across the desert on a camel, think again. Camels won't arrive in Egypt until about 600BC – and won't be used for travel for 300 years after that. Horses are an option, but too expensive for most people. In town, you might be able to rent a chariot – or even a carrying chair – but the distances are so small it's hardly worth it.

Carrying chairs are totally impractical on desert sand.

TOP TIPS FOR TOURISTS

No. 3: Desert storm

NEVER agree to a tour of the desert with a friendly "guide". You'll be robbed before you've gone a few steps. Coming back (if you're left alive), you'll almost certainly get lost. One Persian general lost his entire army in the desert. It was never seen again.

If you venture further afield on land, take a string of donkeys carrying plenty of drinking water. Dehydration (lack of water) is a constant problem. Two pharaohs had wells built on the way to some gold mines in the eastern desert, but it's a long way between oases (pools of water) in the western desert.

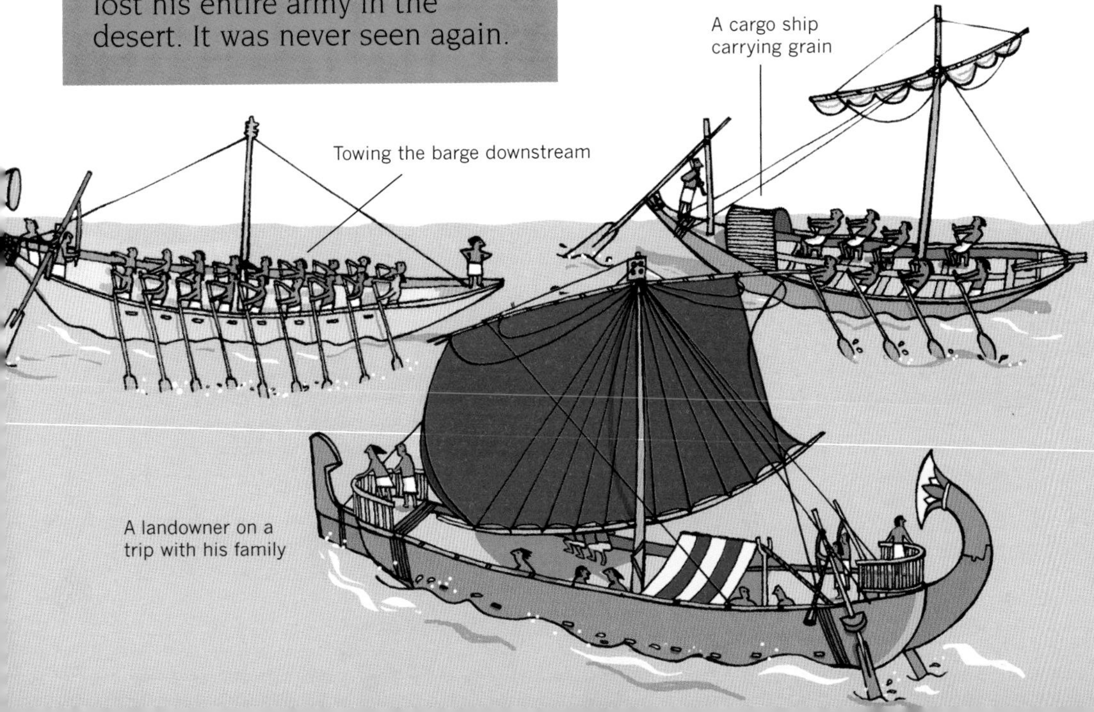

A cargo ship carrying grain

Towing the barge downstream

A landowner on a trip with his family

13

WHERE TO STAY

For most of the vacation, you'll be sleeping on (or beside) a boat. But for your forays onto dry land, there are no hotels and the inns are best avoided: many are simply beer houses with (very) rowdy customers. Your only course of action is to rent somewhere.

TOWN PLANNING

Renting a townhouse or apartment isn't the most restful option. Towns are crowded, busy, noisy and dirty, with buildings crammed together. Most towns sprang up piecemeal. Even the few that are planned don't last, as each generation builds on top of the ones before.

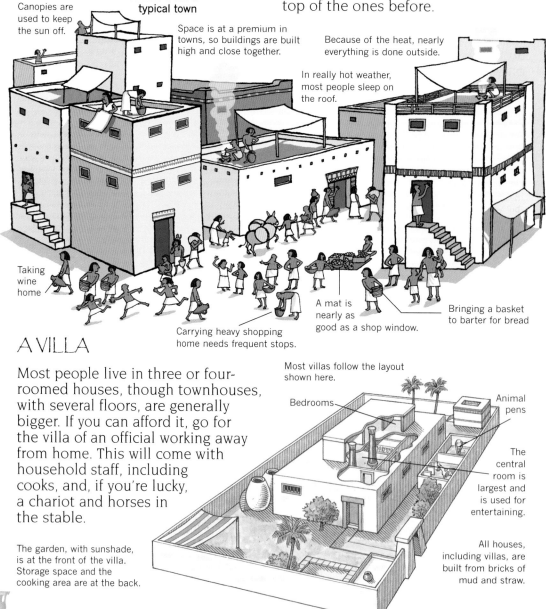

A scene from a typical town

Canopies are used to keep the sun off.

Space is at a premium in towns, so buildings are built high and close together.

Because of the heat, nearly everything is done outside.

In really hot weather, most people sleep on the roof.

Taking wine home

A mat is nearly as good as a shop window.

Bringing a basket to barter for bread

Carrying heavy shopping home needs frequent stops.

A VILLA

Most people live in three or four-roomed houses, though townhouses, with several floors, are generally bigger. If you can afford it, go for the villa of an official working away from home. This will come with household staff, including cooks, and, if you're lucky, a chariot and horses in the stable.

Most villas follow the layout shown here.

Bedrooms

Animal pens

The central room is largest and is used for entertaining.

The garden, with sunshade, is at the front of the villa. Storage space and the cooking area are at the back.

All houses, including villas, are built from bricks of mud and straw.

FURNITURE

There's a limited range of furniture, but it's of a surprisingly modern design and a good standard of craftsmanship. Like everything else in Egypt, the more costly an item, the better it is made and the more expensive the materials used.

Basics include stools, tables, and chairs – though these are only for the most important people in the house. Beds are a wooden frame, with linen sheets. The "pillows" may come as a shock. They're just wooden (or even stone) headrests.

The Egyptians find the headrests very comfortable, but you may prefer to use a cushion.

Oil-burning lamps are decorative – but not very bright.

AIR CONDITIONING

In a country where the heat is intense, only the very rich have air conditioning. In Egypt, this means a servant with a fan. The few concessions to the heat are air vents in the roof, to catch what breeze there is, and tiny windows set high up in the walls, which let in as little sun as possible. Walls are thick and often whitewashed on the outside to reflect the heat.

PUBLIC AMENITIES

There's no state sewage or refuse collection. You'll be throwing your waste into pits (or occasionally the river or street) like everyone else. It's the one time you'll be grateful for the heat. Refuse dries up so quickly that smells don't have a chance to linger. . There's no running water either. All water is collected from private or public wells and carried to the house. If you're exceptionally lucky, your villa will have its own well.

"BATH" ROOM

Better properties have bathrooms, though there are no bathtubs, just a toilet and "shower". Walls are lined with limestone to protect them from splashes, as the shower is a servant pouring a jug of water over you. The toilet, though, is a wooden seat over a large clay pot filled with sand. The pot is taken away to be emptied.

TOP TIPS FOR TOURISTS

No. 4: Feeling lost?

Try not to be confused by the lack of street names and numbers. Egyptians find their way around with reference to other buildings near the place they want to go. Get into the habit of memorizing the location of useful landmarks.

15

FOOD & DRINK

If you take a vacation for a rest from cooking, you're in for a letdown. In Egypt, you'll be self-catering. There are no cafés, only a few snack stands offering bread, meat and beer. If you can't cook, or don't want to slave over a hot fire without a dozen electrical gadgets on hand, rent a villa with servants to do it for you.

BREAD AND BEER

Bread and beer, made from wheat and/or barley, are the staples of everyone's diet, no matter what their age or class. It's made Egyptian bakers inventive – you'll find more than 40 types of bread and cakes on offer. Bread often comes with added extras, such as honey, garlic or herbs.

Even peasants have a better diet than other ancient peoples, because Egypt's agriculture is so rich. For the wealthier Egyptian or tourist, the choice is wider still. The cooking oil, made from linseed, saffron, sesame and sometimes olives, adds a distinctive taste to dishes. So does honey – used to sweeten things as there's no sugar.

This mountain of food from a tomb painting shows onions, pomegranates, cucumbers, grapes, ducks and fish – the diet of a wealthy Egyptian.

MEAT EATERS

Meat includes mutton, goat and pork (unless you're a priest). Beef is available, but expensive and only for special occasions. As there's little grazing land, the cows are small, so mainly kept for milk, which is used for cheese. There's a huge variety of fish and fowl, fresh and dried. But don't look for chickens. They're such rare birds, the pharaoh exhibits them in his private zoo.

VEGETARIANS

Fruit and vegetables grow in abundance and include beans, lentils, radishes, garlic, peas, grapes, figs, pomegranates and dates – so you certainly won't lack variety if you don't eat meat. There are also plenty of eggs, nuts and cheese for protein.

TOP TIPS FOR TOURISTS

No. 5: Toothpick

Be careful when you're eating bread. It's made outside and the dough picks up no end of grit and stones – which are then baked in along with the seeds. Not only does this wear down your teeth, you may end up losing a few.

16

A drinking straw

DRINKS

Beer is made from crumbled bread and water, and so lumpy it's strained before serving. More expensive is the wine, made from dates, grapes or pomegranates. Wine labels give the vineyard, year of production and a comment, such as "very, very good".

Apart from beer and wine, there's water. This is safe to drink, either from wells or, amazingly, straight from the Nile. There are no ice cubes, so, to cool the water down, simply let it drip from one clay pot into another.

Beer is drunk through large wooden straws with filters. Even after straining, it remains full of lumps.

COOKING

Because of the heat and fire risk, all cooking takes place outside. If you take turns cooking, bear in mind that only women bake bread.

FAN THE FLAMES

Large joints of meat are turned on a spit, often over a brazier (metal container) filled with charcoal. The most common fuels though are sticks, dried grass and reeds. Reeds give short, sharp bursts of heat, but need constant fanning to keep alight.

Cooking al fresco

Most Egyptians cook on a tripod (three-legged stand) over a fire.

66 I have been over this blaze since the world began. I never saw such a [huge] duck! 99

XII Dynasty cook

Loaves are formed into rounds and stuck on the outside of the oven. They fall off when cooked.

To keep a fire going, someone has to fan the flames. (It helps if someone fans him.)

17

GETTING SICK

Ancient Egypt isn't a bad place to be if you're ill. The Egyptians' belief in hygiene and their logical approach to medicine reach a standard not seen again until the 1800s (AD). That said, it's better to have an obvious problem, such as a gashed arm, than appendicitis.

Egyptian doctors have a widespread reputation for excellence, some working as far afield as Babylon. Most work as general practitioners, though there are also specialists who focus on specific parts of the body.

VISITING A DOCTOR

Much like home, doctors observe symptoms, ask questions and examine their patients before making a diagnosis. Everything is recorded on papyrus (the Egyptian form of paper), so there's a record for the future. These notes are stored in vast medical libraries in temples, which doctors are free to consult. If your doctor hasn't a clue, he'll be upfront about that too.

SURGERY

If you need an operation, your chances of survival are fairly high. Instruments are always sterilized in flames and surgeons keep both their patients and surroundings clean. Fractures are healed with splints and casts, and open wounds are closed with stitches and clamps. There's even an anesthetic made from poppies, which doubles as a painkiller.

A knife used in surgery and a pair of iron tweezers

A TEXTBOOK CASE

What in later years will become known as the "Edwin Smith" papyrus has 48 case studies, and may date back to the Third Dynasty. Doctors use it to check a range of complaints from wounds to fractures.

66 This is an ailment I can treat. This is an ailment I will try to treat. This is an ailment not to be treated. 99

You'll hear one of these three statements before diagnosis.

One king brought his entire family over from Canaan, just to consult an Egyptian doctor.

MEDICAL MANUALS

There are papyruses on surgery, anatomy and pharmacy (the use of drugs). All drugs are natural (animal, plant or mineral-based) and some are surprisingly effective. In fact, Nile mud, a popular ingredient, has an antibiotic in it.

MEDICINE & RELIGION

All treatment, even for a broken limb, involves prayer. The Egyptians are highly religious and believe that everything they do should have the blessing of the gods. If all else fails, go to a temple and ask to sleep there. You may not undergo a miraculous recovery, but with luck you'll dream the cure.

Even if you dream a cure, you may still need a priest to interpret its meaning.

INTERNAL ORGANS

Much of the knowledge doctors have of internal organs comes from mummification (the technique used to preserve a body after death). Doctors know that the heart pumps blood and say of the pulse, "It speaks the messages of the heart." But they vastly overrate the heart's importance. They believe it the source of intelligence, ignoring the brain. They even think that the stomach is connected to the heart.

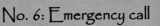

> **“** O... Isis... come and see your father concerning that enemy, dead man or dead woman, which is in the head of N... **”**

A charm for curing a headache caused by a spirit inside the head

TOP TIPS FOR TOURISTS

No. 6: Emergency call

As a last resort, call on a god associated with healing, such as **Thoth, Isis, Sekhmet** or **Imhotep**, and leave a *stela* (a piece of stone with a prayer on it) at a temple.

Stelae* are often covered in ears – a pointed reminder to the gods to listen to the pleas written on them.

*Stelae is the plural of stela

THE GREAT PYRAMIDS

First stop on the river cruise is one of the most spectacular sights you'll see, on this trip or any other – the Great Pyramids, already over 1,000 years old. Located at **Gizah**, they're a popular day out for the Ancient Egyptians too.

They were built for three pharaohs of the Fourth Dynasty (Khufu, Khafre and Menkaure; also known as Cheops, Chephren and Mycerinus) as giant tombs for their mummified bodies.

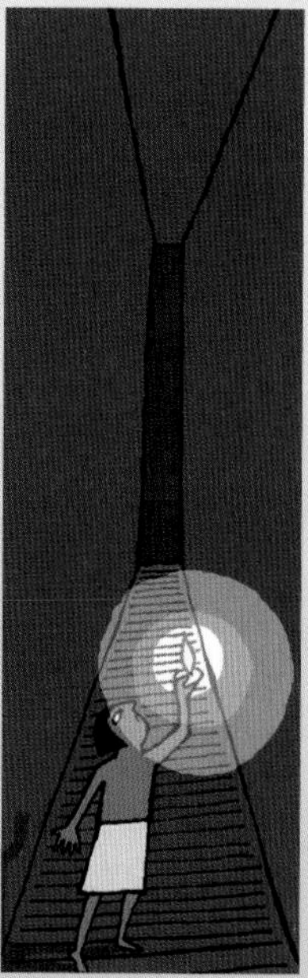

PYRAMID FACTS

The largest pyramid was built for Khufu c.2500BC. At 140m (460ft) tall, it's taller than 24 giraffes on top of each other, and contains more than 2.5 million blocks. These were cut so precisely, the gaps between them are less than 0.5mm (1/32 inch) wide. The pyramid is encased in limestone which gleams a dazzling white in the sun.

The Grand Gallery: a shaft leading to Khufu's chamber (see diagram on right)

THE WORKFORCE

A pyramid took about 20 years to build, but it wasn't built by suffering slaves. The builders were free men and, though it was hard work, each man only worked on the project for a short time. Besides, he was fed, clothed and housed by the king; the work reduced his tax bill; and it pleased the gods.

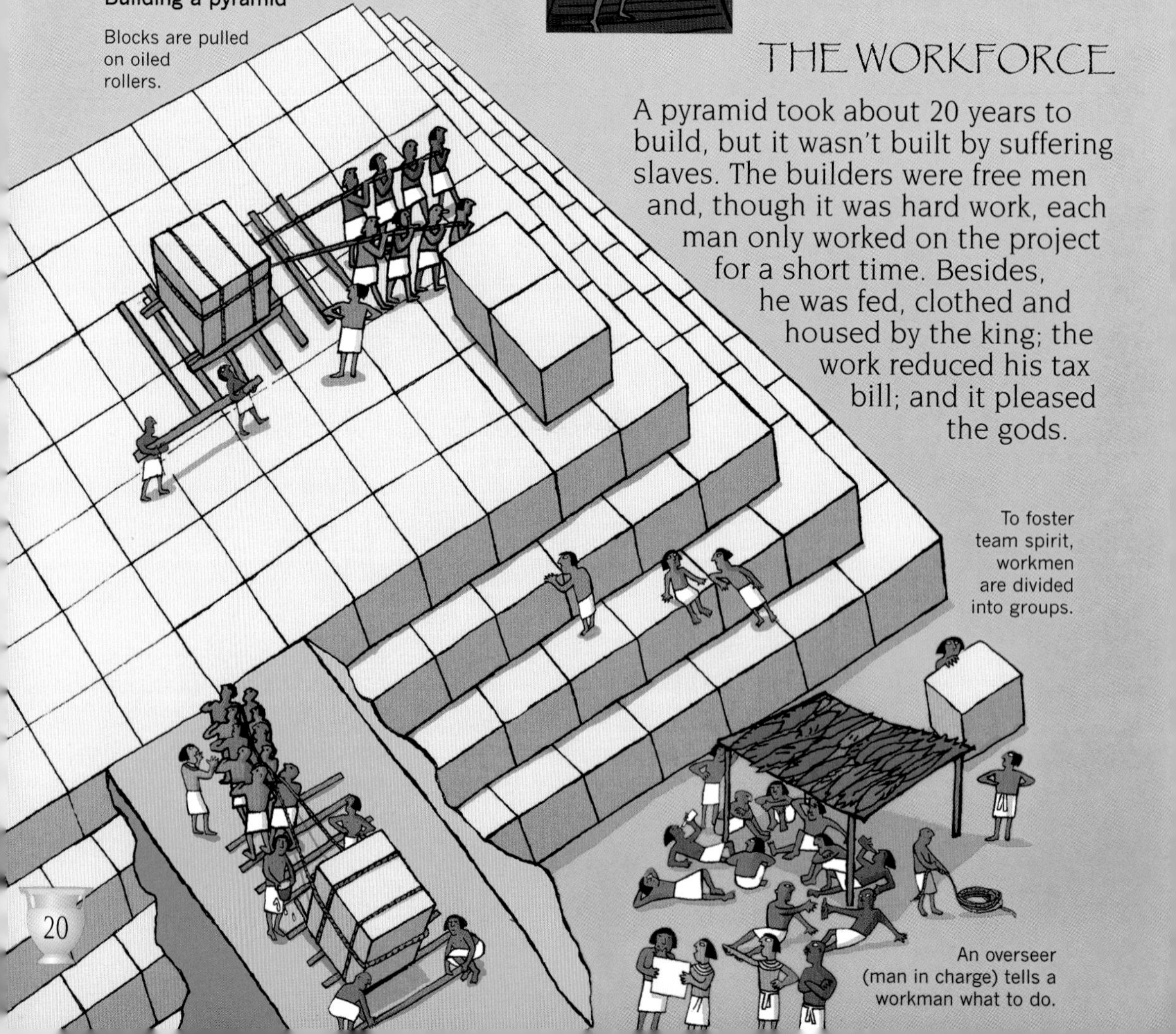

Building a pyramid

Blocks are pulled on oiled rollers.

To foster team spirit, workmen are divided into groups.

An overseer (man in charge) tells a workman what to do.

TOMB ROBBERS

Egyptians believe in a life after death, so pharaohs are buried with everything they might need in that next life, plus numerous valuables. It means the pyramids are – or were – a treasure trove. Huge stone blocks were used to seal off their entrances but, spurred on by the thought of all that gold, thieves got in anyway. Even now, halfway through the New Kingdom, most pyramids have been cleaned out.

The wall of Khufu's pyramid has been cut away to show inside.

Five chambers spread the weight of the stones above.

Khufu's chamber

Empty chamber

Empty chamber

The Grand Gallery: 48m (157ft) long and 8.5m (28ft) high

PYRAMID TEMPLES

Upon arrival at the pyramids, you may well moor near to the Valley Temple on the bank of the Nile. This is where the pharaoh's body was brought on its final journey from the palace. The body was carried down the Nile in a *barque* (funeral boat), which was then buried beside the pyramid.

A covered road links the Valley Temple with a second temple, the Mortuary Temple, built in front of the pyramid. For hundreds of years, this temple was visited daily by priests with food for the dead pharaoh to sustain him in the afterlife.

The Sphinx, whose face is said to have been based on King Khafre's

TOP TIPS FOR TOURISTS

No. 7: Souvenirs

Don't buy anything from one of the many sellers hawking "genuine" souvenirs outside the pyramids. One: it's illegal. Two: whether they're pyramid stone or "royal jewels", they're undoubtedly fakes.

GUARDIAN OF GIZAH

Standing guard over the pyramids, though not that effectively, is the enigmatic Sphinx. At the start of the New Kingdom, it was buried under sand. You'll see it on your trip thanks to a young prince (later Tuthmosis IV), who dreamed if he cleared it, he would be king.

STEP PYRAMIDS

Think of a pyramid and you'll probably picture the straight-sided ones at Gizah, pointing to the sky. But your next stop off, **Sakkara**, is home to some different pyramids, the first ever built.

Sakkara, south of Gizah, is the necropolis (cemetery) for Memphis, the capital of the Old Kingdom. The largest of the cemeteries, it contains 15 royal pyramids. King of them all is the one built for Djoser, a pharaoh at the start of the Third Dynasty.

SIX STEPS TO HEAVEN

Originally, pharaohs were buried in mud-brick buildings called *mastabas*. Then, Djoser's architect, Imhotep, designed a tomb made of stone that would revolutionize burials.

Taking a stone mastaba as his starting point, he enlarged it and built five more on top, each one smaller than the one beneath. This formed a "step" pyramid of six layers, popularly said to represent the pharaoh's stepladder to heaven.

A step pyramid

The buildings around the edge are finely carved on the outside, but the insides are full of rubble.

The "Heb Sed" court, where the king celebrates the festival of "Sed" (see page 55).

The pyramid is set in a vast complex, 547m (1,790ft) by 278m (912ft). Most of the other buildings are for decoration only.

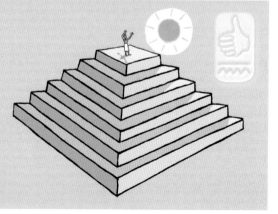

TOP TIPS FOR TOURISTS

No. 8: Steps to prison

Tempting though the steps may be, don't try to climb them (as tourists from later centuries will). It's the height of disrespect and you could end up somewhere that's the very opposite of heaven.

PYRAMID TEXTS

Look out especially for Unas' pyramid. (Unas was a pharaoh of the Fifth Dynasty.) If you can get inside, do. The interior walls were the first to be covered in hieroglyphic messages, containing chants and spells. These were meant to protect and help the pharaoh on his hazardous journey through *Duat* (the underworld) to the afterlife.

Stonemasons painstakingly carve text onto the interior walls of a tomb.

FROM STONE TO PAPER

These wall spells, known as *Pyramid Texts*, were strictly for pharaohs only. Years later, the idea was adopted by private individuals, who painted charms onto their coffins. These were termed *Coffin Texts*. Since the beginning of the New Kingdom, they have been inscribed on sheets of papyrus and are called the *Book of the Dead* (see page 37).

"LIVING" CEMETERY

Sakkara is more than a site for ancient pyramids though. You may see a burial taking place during your visit. (In fact, it will go on being used as a cemetery right up to the 21st century AD.)

All the tombs are decorated with wall paintings and painted reliefs (wall carvings).

A NOBLE GRAVEYARD

Some of the mastabas just north of Djoser's pyramid go back even earlier, to the First Dynasty. But these belong to various nobles and court officials. First and Second Dynasty pharaohs were buried in a royal cemetery at Abydos, close to the town of Thebes in Upper Egypt.

Kings only began to be buried at Sakkara from the start of the Third Dynasty, when the royal burial ground was moved here. These pharaohs' tombs are surrounded by hundreds of others, belonging to members of the royal household and their families.

Currently, pharaohs are buried in the **Valley of the Kings** on the West Bank (see pages 28-29) but some officials are still entombed here. If, during your visit, a tomb is being prepared for one of Ramesses' courtiers, you may even get the chance to look around inside.

Tomb walls show scenes from everyday life, such as boat builders hard at work.

THE SIGHTS OF MEMPHIS

Halfway between the burial sites of Sakkara and Gizah lies **Memphis**, Egypt's capital during the Old Kingdom. Still the country's key administrative headquarters, Memphis is at the heart of Egypt's thriving import/export industry. It's grown since Menes founded it – see how small it was by following the dazzling white walls which enclosed the early city. You can easily spend several days here, if you can stand the noise. There's masses to see and buy, cheap imports in particular.

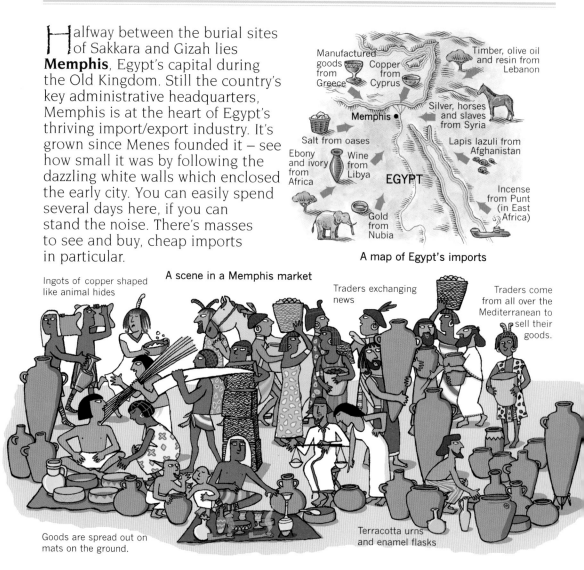

Manufactured goods from Greece

Copper from Cyprus

Timber, olive oil and resin from Lebanon

Silver, horses and slaves from Syria

Memphis •

Salt from oases

Ebony and ivory from Africa

Wine from Libya

EGYPT

Lapis lazuli from Afghanistan

Incense from Punt (in East Africa)

Gold from Nubia

A map of Egypt's imports

A scene in a Memphis market

Ingots of copper shaped like animal hides

Traders exchanging news

Traders come from all over the Mediterranean to sell their goods.

Goods are spread out on mats on the ground.

Terracotta urns and enamel flasks

FOREIGN TRADE

Just below the Nile Delta, Memphis is in the perfect spot for trade. Many traders settle here, giving the city a cosmopolitan feel. Mingling with the merchants you'll find everyone from foreign dignitaries bearing gold tributes for the king, to peasants from oases with blocks of salt, and rushes for baskets.

Visit the docks to see boats being loaded with papyrus and linen for export by *shwty* (government traders). Imports include cedar from the Lebanon – vital in view of Egypt's lack of tall trees. There are even shrines for foreign gods, an example of the Egyptians' liberal "Pray and let pray" attitude to religion.

THE TEMPLE OF PTAH

As you'd expect of so great a city, Memphis has its own god – and not just any god. According to Memphisians, their god Ptah (say "tar") created the world by saying the name of each thing in turn, bringing it to life. Whether you believe this or not, his temple is one of the largest in Egypt.

The god Ptah creating life

South of the temple is an enclosure where you can see the famous **Apis bull** – believed to be Ptah in an earthly form. (Gods are so powerful, they can't be seen in their true form, so an animal is chosen for the god's spirit to reside in.) Each time the bull dies, all of Egypt is scoured for a replacement. The lucky bull that fits the correct description gets to live like a god.

The Apis bull is always black and white, with a white pyramid on his forehead and a vulture-shaped patch on his back.

HELIOPOLIS

Only a short boat ride away, and definitely worth the trip, is the town of **Heliopolis**. It houses the temple of Re the Sun God. This temple is open to let in the sun, so you'll get a good view. Look for the obelisk in the third courtyard, with a copy of the "Benben" stone at the top. Said to be a gift from Re, the stone fell flaming from the sky (so it's probably a meteorite). You may even see Re himself. Like Ptah, his earthly form is a bull, known as the **Mnevis bull**.

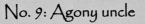

The obelisk topped with a copy of the Benben stone

TOP TIPS FOR TOURISTS

No. 9: Agony uncle

Something worrying you? Visit the Apis bull. You can ask him any question you like, as long as the answer is *yes* or *no*. Go to the courtyard where the bull is to be paraded (follow the crowd) and give a priest your question. In front of the bull stand identical feeding troughs, marked *Yes* and *No*. When the priest asks your question, the trough the bull eats from gives your answer.

TEMPLES

Your next major stop after Memphis is **Thebes**, religious capital of the New Kingdom (and known to the Egyptians as *Waset*). Thebes is a place you'll want to stay in for several days. Whether it's tombs or temples which interest you, Thebes and nearby **Karnak** have the most magnificent you'll see anywhere.

TEMPLE OF AMUN

The **Temple of Amun** at Karnak, dedicated to the king of the gods, is king of all temples. Begun in the Middle Kingdom, it has been extended by each dynasty of the New Kingdom. (Ramesses II has craftily taken the credit for work completed by previous pharaohs.) It will continue to be added to, well into the first century BC.

Ramesses II himself has added a vast *pylon*, or gateway, which leads to the renowned *hypostyle* hall. This has 134 columns, some 21m (70ft) tall. Look for the carvings on the outer walls, showing Ramesses II and his father in battle.

A distracted priest with his animal skin on back to front

The pillars are carved with scenes of pharaohs making offerings to the gods.

TOP TIPS FOR TOURISTS

No. 10: Shhh!

Be very quiet when making an offering or praying at a temple. Don't draw attention to yourself. The gods can hear you perfectly well – and no one else wants to.

LUXOR TEMPLE

South of Karnak is **Luxor**, a smaller, simpler temple, though no less impressive. It's here that the annual festival of **Opet** takes place (see page 55). Amenhotep III built the temple in 1380BC. Ramesses is currently adding a pylon gate, a courtyard and his trademark: huge statues. At the entrance stand two huge obelisks, though by the 19th century only one will remain. The other will be sent to Paris in 1831.

The Temple of Luxor

An avenue of sphinxes leads from Karnak to Luxor.

A TEMPLE LAYOUT

Every town or village has at least one temple, dedicated to a particular god. Some temples are vast complexes, others are more basic, but they all have the same layout. At the entrance is an open courtyard – which is as far as most people get. For those allowed in, a *hypostyle* hall leads to the shrine.

KEEP OUT!

Theoretically, the only person who can make offerings to the gods is the pharaoh, a god himself. In practice, he delegates to priests. So, as a rule, only the pharaoh and his priests – the servants of a god – may enter a temple.

Shrine with a statue of the temple's god

Inside a temple

Obelisk

Hypostyle hall

Courtyard

School room, workshops and storerooms

Sacred pool where priests get water to purify themselves

27

The pyramids proved too spectacular for their own good: they were all robbed. So, for over 200 years, kings have been buried in secret tombs in the **Valley of the Kings**. These are in cliffs at West Thebes, on the edge of the western desert. The area is dominated by "The Peak", a pyramid-shaped mountain on which the deadly cobra goddess *Merit-Seger* is said to live. She resents intruders – but tomb robbers don't give up easily.

BUILDING A TOMB

The tomb site for each pharaoh is chosen soon after he takes the throne, and work begins immediately. Plans are drawn up and orders are sent to the workers. If you go to watch them, take plenty of water. Loose rock and sand are dug out with chisels and wooden mallets and it's a dusty business. The work is hot and tiring and space is limited, so don't get in the way.

Tomb builders hard at work

Tombs are lit by linen wicks burning in saucers of animal fat.

TOP TIPS FOR TOURISTS

No. 11: Stop thief!

Don't wander around alone. Guards are on constant patrol. Anyone not at work is treated with suspicion. To be on the safe side, offer the Medjay a gift and ask for a tour.

As well as the diggers, there are workers checking that the walls, roof and floors are straight, porters dragging baskets of stone away, and painters and plasterers hard at work. Occasionally, sheets of polished metal are used to reflect sunlight into the tombs, making the tombs brighter. It's an impressive trick if you can find someone with the time to show you.

"THE VILLAGE"

If you spend a few days exploring the area, you'll probably stay in **The Village** (Deir El-Medina in modern times). It's the purpose-built estate for the tomb workers, with the Valley of the Kings on one side and the **Valley of the Queens** on the other.

The path between the tombs and estate is a difficult trek, so workers sleep in huts by the tombs for the working week, returning home to their families for the weekend. You could rent a worker's house, though they tend to be airless with little light. (Windows are simply tiny slits by the ceiling.)

Stairs lead to the roof where the worker's family spends most of the day.

A cutaway of a worker's house

This house is one in a row of mud-brick terraces.

This wooden model, covered in gold, shows the pharaoh Tutankhamun on a raft, about to throw a harpoon.

FAMOUS RESIDENT

You can't enter the tomb of **Tutankhamun** (a pharaoh of the previous dynasty) but a guard may point out its entrance. He's the pharaoh everyone will be able to name in 3,000 years' time, but he wasn't that important in his day. He was simply the "boy-king", who died young after a short reign. What makes him special is that he'll reach the 20th century AD with his tomb more or less intact, and the treasures buried with him are fantastic.

A detail from the head of a couch, left in the tomb for Tutankhamun to rest upon

TOMB ART

Called "Place of Beauty" by the Egyptians, the **Valley of the Queens** is the burial site for the pharaohs' wives and offspring. The major tomb currently being built here is for Nefertari, chief wife of Ramesses II. Try to visit it if you can – but you'll need to be persuasive with the workmen. Some of the finest examples of Egyptian art are found in tombs. Nefertari's will be one of the best.

Antechamber

A plan of Nefertari's tomb

The tomb was designed to mirror Nefertari's journey through the afterlife: the stairs represent her descent into the underworld.

Burial chamber

One of three annexes which will become a storehouse for treasure

The walls and pillars show Nefertari with gods and goddesses, a common theme for New Kingdom royal tombs. Non-royal tombs tend to show daily life.

ANCIENT ART

To the Egyptians, art isn't mere representation. Images of people or objects don't just show them, they can replace them. In other words, a picture of fruit on your tomb wall is as good as having the fruit itself. Because of this, an artist aims to tell you as much about the subject as possible. This means Egyptian paintings don't always look that realistic.

A painting of a box with things inside, shows the things on top, so you can see what they are. No object overlaps another, so no detail is hidden from view. Different viewpoints are also combined, the most obvious example being people, who are drawn with their faces in profile but their shoulders full on.

A bearer with offerings from a wall painting on a tomb at Thebes

PAINTING A TOMB

To paint a tomb, plasterers first smooth the walls with clay and apply a layer of plaster. A carefully measured grid is painted on top, using string dipped in red paint. Teams of artists do the first sketch in red, following a plan drawn on squared papyrus. A master artist then corrects mistakes in black ink.

Wall carvings are common in royal tombs. You'll probably see a sculptor carving around the outlines to make them stand out. At this stage, the wall is covered in another, finer layer of plaster before the scenes are painted. Finally, the outlines are gone over once more and details are added with a fine brush.

The different stages of tomb painting

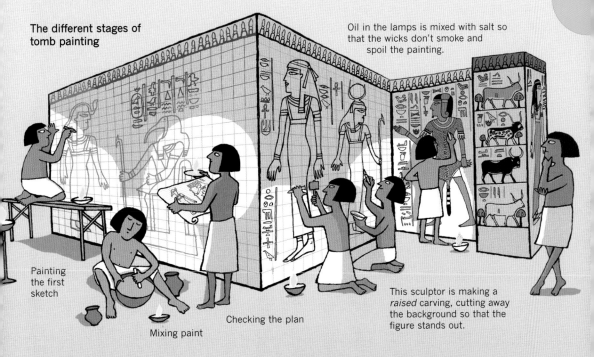

Oil in the lamps is mixed with salt so that the wicks don't smoke and spoil the painting.

Painting the first sketch

Mixing paint

Checking the plan

This sculptor is making a *raised* carving, cutting away the background so that the figure stands out.

MIXING PAINT

Paints are made from minerals such as clay and iron oxide (ochre which gives reds and yellows); malachite (greens); silica, copper and calcium (blue); soot (black) and limestone (white). The dry minerals are pounded to a powder with a pestle and mortar and mixed with gum or egg white to make them liquid.

PERFECT PEOPLE

People are generally shown in an idealized fashion, because this is how they want to look in the afterlife. Study the paintings of Egyptian figures and you'll notice they all look alike. Men and women are always 18 squares tall from their hairlines to the soles of their feet, with their features at set points.

GODS & GODDESSES

The gods are considered so glorious and all-powerful, they cannot be seen with the human eye. To get around this, they appear on earth disguised in animal form. The Egyptians have enormous faith in their gods and goddesses, seeking advice, help or approval on a daily basis. They pray to hundreds, both local (who are unheard of outside a particular region) and national.

You can use this page as a quick reference for the main gods you'll come across when visiting tombs.

AMUN-RE

Two gods for the price of one, **Amun-Re** was originally **Re**, Sun God and King of Egypt, and **Amun**, god of Thebes. When Thebes was made the capital of Egypt, the two merged to become chief god and protector of the pharaoh.

TOP TIPS FOR TOURISTS

No. 12: Don't say his name!

Only once, under **Akhenaten**, did Egypt almost become a one-god nation. Akhenaten promoted a sun god, Aten, above all others, but the scheme lasted as long as his reign. His reputation is now so low that the penalty for anyone even saying his name is severe.

OSIRIS

Osiris is the King of the Underworld and the second most important god. He was the first to die and live again, the ambition of every Egyptian. His temple is at Abydos where he is said to have been buried.

THE STORY OF OSIRIS

Osiris was one of the earliest kings of Egypt. Much beloved, he taught his people how to grow crops. But he was tricked and murdered by his jealous brother Set. Osiris's sister-wife Isis found his body but, when she returned with it, Set simply cut it up. Refusing to give in, Isis collected every part. With the help of Anubis, she mummified Osiris and brought him back to life.

Osiris

Today, all mummies are prepared in the same way, in the hope that they, too, will come back to life. Osiris's face was even painted green to symbolize regrowth and rebirth. Figures of Osiris, made from mud and sown with wheat seed, are often left in tombs. It's thought that the new life, growing in the form of wheat, will be extra encouragement.

Amun-Re

BEST OF THE REST

Isis: devoted sister-wife of Osiris and protector of women, Egyptian women look up to her as a model wife and mother. In recent times, her importance has grown.

Set: Osiris's evil brother, he's god of trouble, the desert and storms. Animals associated with him are pigs, donkeys and male hippos.

Horus: son of Osiris and Isis, he inherited the throne after his father's death. (Now, all kings become the living embodiment of Horus on ascending the throne.) Sometimes shown with a falcon's head, his main temple is at Edfu.

Hathor: Horus's wife. Currently eclipsed by Isis, she's an important, ancient goddess of music, beauty and love. Her sacred animal is a cow.

Bes: a dwarf and the jester of the gods, he also looks the most approachable. He protects the house and family, especially children. Though he has no temple of his own, there are models of him in most homes.

Tawaret: a pregnant hippo, who, as you'd expect, is the goddess of pregnancy and childbirth.

Ma'at: goddess of truth and justice, harmony and the balance of the Universe. She's usually shown in human form but sometimes represented by a feather.

Anubis: jackal-headed god of the dead and mummification, and guardian of cemeteries. (Jackals look like dogs.)

Thoth: god of the moon, wisdom and healing, and patron of scribes (officials who can write). Mathematicians, engineers and officials all worship Thoth. According to legend, he wrote 42 volumes containing all the wisdom in the world.

Ptah: the god of craftsmen, whose main temple is at Memphis. He's married to Sekhmet.

Sekhmet: the goddess who avenges wrongs done to Re. A destructive and feared deity, she also cures disease with her breath.

A MUMMY FACTORY

Conjure up an image of Ancient Egypt and you'll probably picture mummies, the embalmed (preserved) bodies of dead Egyptians. Though, strictly speaking, a tour around a "mummy factory" isn't available to visitors, doors will open in return for a "gift".

WHY A "MUMMY"?

All Egyptians believe life continues after death. But, to enjoy the afterlife fully, their bodies must survive. This need for a body after death led to mummification, a drying out of the body to preserve it. Don't call them mummies, though. The name will only catch on when they're discovered in the 19th century AD. The mummies' blackened skin (from embalming resin) made their Arab discoverers believe they'd been coated in *mummiya*, a kind of tar.

LAND OF THE DEAD

Soon after death, bodies are taken to the west bank of the Nile. This desert area where the sun sets is thought of as the land of the dead. Here, they are washed and purified before being taken to a building, the *wabet*, to be embalmed. If you get into a wabet, be respectful. You are watching a sacred rite, after all.

Unless you have a couple of months, you'll have to see the various stages of embalming on different bodies. Proper embalming takes up to 70 days, though services range from deluxe to very cheap. The poor are preserved in less than a week.

TOP TIPS FOR TOURISTS

No.13: An iron stomach

Even grown men pale at the sight of someone's brains being pulled through their nostrils. Plan your visit carefully, that is, not just before or after lunch.

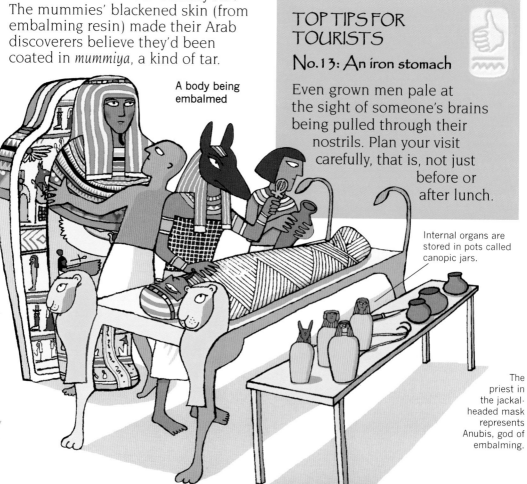

A body being embalmed

Internal organs are stored in pots called canopic jars.

The priest in the jackal-headed mask represents Anubis, god of embalming.

A BEGINNER'S GUIDE...

Workers called *wetyw* (bandagers) first coat the head in resin to preserve it and remove the brain, which they throw away. The stomach, intestines, liver and lungs are removed through a cut on the left-hand side of the abdomen and mummified separately.

The heart is left intact, or replaced with a *scarab* (a charm of a sacred beetle) if it's accidentally damaged. The body is then rinsed, packed with stuffing and left in natron (a moisture-absorbing salt) for up to 40 days.

A finished mummy with a painted face

Mummies are wrapped in up to 20 layers of bandages, glued together with resin.

66 My corpse is permanent, it will not perish nor be destroyed in this land for ever. 99

Spell 154, from the Book of the Dead

AFTER DRYING

A dried-out body won't be like any body you've seen. It's much darker, and weighs three-quarters less. Arms and legs are matchstick-thin and the skin is stiff and hangs in folds. At this point, the embalmer's skill comes into its own. The body is emptied, rinsed out and restuffed with resin-soaked linen or sawdust, herbs and spices. It's then massaged with oils to restore the skin's softness. The face is also made up, all to create as lifelike an appearance as possible.

FINISHING TOUCHES

A coat of resin is plastered on and the body is decked with jewels. Then it's wrapped in bandages and placed in the first of several linen shrouds, layered with amulets (charms) for luck. The final touch is a funeral mask over the head.

ANIMAL MUMMIES

Don't be surprised to see animals being embalmed, from cats and dogs to crocodiles; baboons to beetles. This isn't so Egyptians' pets can join them in the next world, but because certain animals are believed to be the animal form of a particular god or goddess. (They also make popular souvenirs.)

A mummified dog

DEATH ON THE NILE

Death may be an unusual subject for a vacation guide to dwell on, but you can't escape it in Ancient Egypt. It's not that the Egyptians are morbid – far from it. Attend one of their parties and you'll see they live life to the full. They just believe life on this earth is only the beginning. After death, comes a hazardous journey through Duat, the underworld, to the Field of Reeds in the Other World (heaven).

To ensure a body reaches the Other World intact, the mummy is placed in a protective, human-shaped coffin. Coffins are painted with decorative scenes and magic signs, to help the deceased on the journey to the Field of Reeds. Royalty, who always go several better, don't just have one wooden coffin. They get a whole nest of them – with the inner coffins made of solid gold – plus a sarcophagus (stone coffin) to boot.

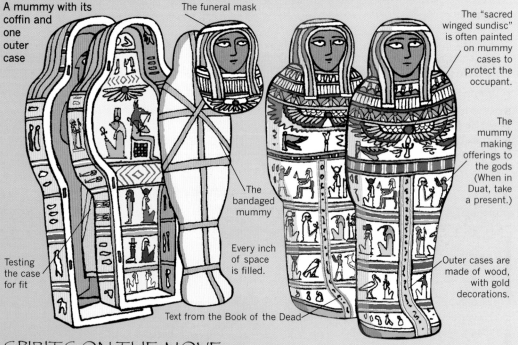

A mummy with its coffin and one outer case

The funeral mask

The "sacred winged sundisc" is often painted on mummy cases to protect the occupant.

The mummy making offerings to the gods (When in Duat, take a present.)

The bandaged mummy

Every inch of space is filled.

Testing the case for fit

Outer cases are made of wood, with gold decorations.

Text from the Book of the Dead

SPIRITS ON THE MOVE

Egyptians believe various spirits are born with a person, and that these have a life of their own after death. The three most important spirits are:

Ka: the life force – a person's physical double. The Ka can move around the tomb, so doors are painted on coffins to let it out.

Ba: a person's character; it roams the earth during the day but returns to the tomb at night.

Akh: a person's immortality; after death, it joins the stars.

Coffins have clear (if flattering) portraits of their occupants, so the Ba can find its body.

BOOK OF THE DEAD

Not content to rely on charms in bandages and symbols on coffins, spells are used to help the dead person pass through Duat safely. In pyramid times, these were carved on tomb walls. Now, the *Book of the Dead* (up to nearly 200 spells written on papyrus) is slipped in a coffin.

Each version of the book is slightly different. The rich have their books custom-made, choosing the spells they think they'll need; poorer customers buy books already written, with a gap for their name.

A scarab charm

WEIGHING THE HEART

A person has to undergo many trials before he can enter the Field of Reeds. One of the most famous spells in the *Book of the Dead* concerns the final trial: Weighing the Heart. Before a jury of 12, the heart is balanced against an ostrich feather, symbol of truth and justice.

If it's too full of wickedness, the heart will outweigh the feather and, in theory, the person is doomed. In practice, a scarab-shaped stone is often put into the body to make sure that, through magic, the person passes the test.

A scene from the Book of the Dead, showing the "Weighing the Heart" ceremony

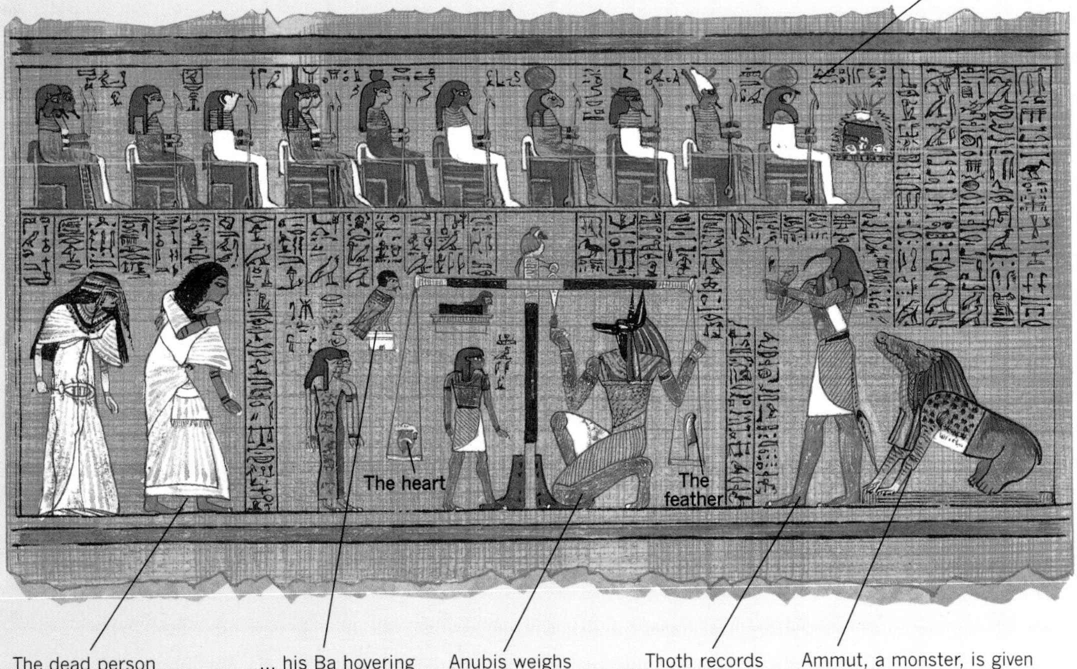

Gods make up the jury.

The heart

The feather

The dead person is shown watching...

... his Ba hovering by the scales.

Anubis weighs the heart.

Thoth records the outcome.

Ammut, a monster, is given the heart if it fails the test.

37

A FUNERAL PROCESSION

With death rates high, if you spend any time at a major tomb site, you're bound to see a funeral. Even the wealthy, who can expect to live longest, rarely make it past their mid-fifties; many don't survive childhood. You may even see the funeral of a prince or princess, since the Pharaoh has dozens of wives and innumerable children.

The long walk to the tomb

Family and friends, priests and professional mourners follow the mummy to the tomb.

THE FINAL JOURNEY

Funerals, for the rich at least, take place 70 days after death. On the day of the funeral, the mourners cross to the West Bank, collecting the mummy on their way to the tomb. Funerals are solemn, but there's nothing gloomy about them. You'll hear the procession long before you see it, the wailing of the professional mourners rising above a constant chanting of prayers.

TOP TIPS FOR TOURISTS

No. 14: See how the other half lives (& dies)

Poorer citizens are buried in the sand with only a few pots and a cheap *shabti* (see right). You may see such a funeral ceremony nearby. The poor often bury their dead by a rich tomb, hoping that some offerings will spill over into their relative's afterlife.

"" Your [tomb] is for eternity... it contains every good thing. ""

An inscription on a stela

Forget funerals back home: here, they are more like moving house. In effect, this is what the dead person is doing. Taking up most of the procession are servants laden with everything the mummy may need in the afterlife: furniture, chests of clothes and food, board games and even slippers.

OPEN WIDE

In the tomb, the chief priest performs a final rite: the Opening of the Mouth ceremony. This restores bodily functions to the mummy, so it can enjoy the afterlife. The priest touches the mummy with special instruments and recites spells. Some tombs contain statues as a spare home for the Ka (the life force spirit) in case anything happens to the mummy. King Khafre had 23 statues, all of which had to have their mouths opened.

A priest in animal skin heads the procession, burning incense.

Oxen drag a sled, which carries the boat-shaped bier (platform for a coffin) on which the mummy lies.

EAT, DRINK & BE MERRY

As well as religious paintings, tomb walls are covered with pictures of food to feed the Ka. In case that isn't enough to satisfy the spirit, fresh food and drink are left too. Tutankhamun was buried with over 100 baskets of fruit. Models of food are thought just as effective. Early Egyptians had entire model bakeries entombed with them.

SHABTIS

Even in paradise, crops have to be sown and canals dug. Initially, the dead were buried with models of their servants. Nowadays, *shabtis* (tiny models of mummies) are used. In years to come, Egyptians with money to burn will have up to 401 shabtis in their tombs: a servant for every day of the year and 36 overseers to keep the servants working.

A shabti (or mini-mummy)

66 O shabti, if the deceased is called upon to do any work [to cultivate the fields or irrigate the river banks] you shall say, "Here I am, I will do it." 99

Spell 6, from the Book of the Dead, inscribed on shabtis

This model boat was left in an early tomb to ensure ample supplies of fish. (It won't work in an empty food cupboard.)

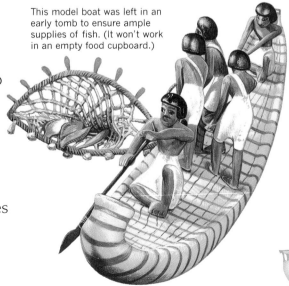

AN EXPEDITION TO NUBIA

On Egypt's southern border lies Nubia. Though less fertile than Egypt, Nubia is rich in natural resources, such as amethysts and gold. Nubia is also the corridor into central Africa with its wealth of ebony and ivory. If you can extend your trip to include a visit here, grab your chance.

Map labels:
EGYPT
Egypt
AFRICA
Nile
Egypt and Africa
Egypt and Africa
Elephantine Island
Aswan
First Cataract
NUBIA
Second Cataract
Under Egyptian control
Third Cataract
Fourth Cataract
Area of Egyptian influence

CHIEF OF CHIEFS

The governor in overall charge of Nubia is called the *King's Son of Kush*. He's assisted by two deputies, one for the north, and one for the south. The region is divided into smaller areas, governed by local chiefs. You may be able to join the party of a new governor, going to Nubia to take up his post.

WAR & PEACE

The history of the Egyptians and Nubians is a troubled one. Eager to protect trade routes and exploit Nubia's resources, the Egyptians have been attacking Nubia since records began. For now, Egypt rules Nubia and there's peace. Egyptian towns and temples have sprung up, and the Nubians have adapted to their occupiers' way of life.

Nubia lies between the First and Second Cataracts (as shown on the larger map). A cataract is where the path of the Nile is blocked by rocks.

ISLAND HOPPING

On the way to Nubia, you'll pass several islands. The one to visit is **Elephantine Island**. On its south-east shore is a Nilometer: a long narrow staircase leading into the Nile. It was built to monitor the country's annual floods. Once officials know how high the Nile has flooded, they can decide whether it will be a good or bad year for crops and set the taxes accordingly.

RAINING GOLD

If you're lucky, you'll see the old governor being fêted at the famous Gold Ceremony. This takes place at the "Window of Appearances", a particular balcony on any one of Ramesses' many palaces. Gold collars are thrown down by the pharaoh to reward loyal and hard-working officials.

Markings on the wall show how high the Nile is flooding.

IVORY MARKET

An official party is bound to call at Elephantine Island, as it's the site of the main market for **Aswan**, a city near the Nubian border. The market is a useful port of call if you need to stock up on anything. Its main trade, though, was once in ivory, which may be how Elephantine Island got its name.

An ivory game piece from the First Dynasty

TOP TIPS FOR TOURISTS

No. 15: Split the cost

If there's an official trip to Nubia and money's tight, you could sign on as a deckhand for the voyage. (Get clearance from the guards first!) Or ask around to see if a minor official (such as a scribe) is willing to go halves on renting a boat. You can share the costs of the trip and camp on board.

NUBIAN MINES

Heating crushed rock to extract the gold

Workers blow on the fire to make it hotter.

A Nubian gold mine

Soldiers run and guard the camp.

Working at the rock face

Most of Egypt's gold comes from Nubia. As you sail upriver, you'll be near the sites of several gold and copper mines. If you're with a new governor, he's certain to stop off and journey into the desert to inspect them. Visiting a camp, you'll be glad you're only a tourist. Mining is backbreaking work and life is hard for the prisoners of war and criminals who work in the mines.

BUHEN FORT & THE ARMY

Visiting Nubia you're ideally placed to see an Egyptian fort. Around the Second Cataract is a string of nine, built in the Middle Kingdom to monitor traffic between Egypt and Nubia. Forts fall into two categories: "plains" and "cataract". Plains forts are much larger, generally rectangular, and built in open spaces. Cataract ones are smaller and irregular shapes (even triangular) to fit their environment.

BUHEN FORT

The plains fort at **Buhen** is one of the most elaborate, with an outer wall of over 8 million bricks. It's more than 700m (2,310ft) long, 8m (26ft) high and 4m (13ft) thick. This surrounds an inner wall, which is even higher and thicker. Behind the walls lies an entire town, with barracks, officers' homes, granaries, storerooms, workshops and stables.

The town is laid out in a grid pattern. Paved streets run between the buildings connecting with a street which runs all the way around the inner wall.

WEAPONS

Soldiers have a wide range of weapons at their disposal, from bows and arrows to swords, the recently introduced scimitars, axes and maces (clubs). In practice though, each unit tends to specialize in one, becoming master of the sword, say, rather than average with them all. Proficiency with weapons is essential: a soldier's only protection comes from his wooden shield, plus a padded jerkin, or leather bands fixed to his tunic, if he's lucky.

A scimitar

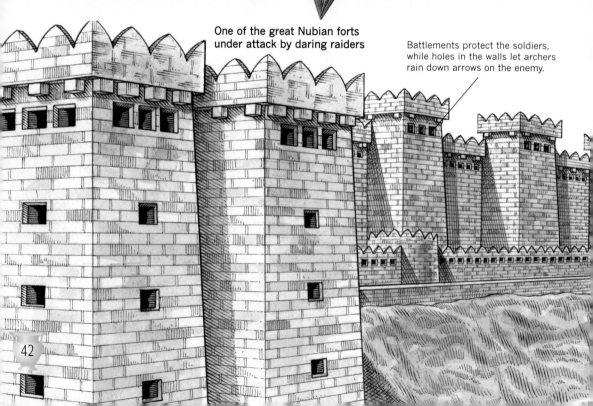

One of the great Nubian forts under attack by daring raiders

Battlements protect the soldiers, while holes in the walls let archers rain down arrows on the enemy.

SOLDIER SOLDIER

The current large professional army, vital to conquer an empire, dates from only the last dynasty. Before that, the army was simply royal bodyguards, supported by trained peasants made to fight in a crisis. Now, soldiers from all classes volunteer. A career in the army offers wealth and adventure.

Soldiers are infantry (foot soldiers), or charioteers.

Charioteers come from the upper class (because of the cost of chariots and horses), but a poor family background won't prevent a boy from rising through the ranks.

CAMPAIGNS

A military expedition is an impressive sight. Added to the thousands of soldiers, there's quite an entourage of scouts, messengers, doctors, priests, cooks, grooms and servants, not forgetting the scribes who organize supplies and keep a daily record, and the hundreds of donkeys carrying bags and tents.

ARMY DIVISIONS

Heading the army is the pharaoh, who often accompanies his men on campaigns. Under him, generals and officers control the ranks. Men are grouped into **divisions** of 5,000, comprising 4,000 infantry and 500 two-man chariots. Each division, named after a god such as Amun or Re, has 20 **companies** of 200 infantrymen and 25 chariots. The infantry are subdivided into **units** of 50 men. Each company has its own name and battle standard.

Forts are sited on hills, where possible, to make life more difficult for the attackers.

The upper walls have an overhang to allow soldiers to drop missiles on the attackers – if they dare leave their cover.

The enemy is ready to fire the second an Egyptian soldier pokes his head over the wall.

43

ABU SIMBEL

To Ramesses II, size is *everything*. Nowhere is this more apparent than at his massive temple at **Abu Simbel**. It was built to impress the Nubians with the pharaoh's power and dedicated to Amun-Re, the sun god Re-Harakhte and Ptah – plus Ramesses himself of course. With the entrance cut into a cliff face, the body of the temple goes deep into the rock.

SEATED GUARDS

As you approach, you'll be greeted by four gigantic statues of Ramesses on his throne. At 20m (65ft) high, they really are colossal.

Hieroglyphs are painted all over the temple's facade.

Figures of Ramesses' family stand between the four statues, barely reaching their calves. Look out for the row of 22 stone baboons above the statues, beside a statue of Re-Harakhte (too small to see in the picture above). Baboons are thought wise because they seem to worship Re. Early Egyptians had noticed wild baboons racing up a cliff face at dawn and raising their paws to the sun. In fact, they were trying to warm themselves.

The statues are brightly painted, standing out against the desert rocks.

All four statues of Ramesses II wear the double crown of Upper and Lower Egypt.

The smaller statue on the left is of Nefertari, Ramesses' chief wife.

INSIDE THE TEMPLE

You're very unlikely to be allowed inside the temple (a right reserved for priests and the pharaoh alone) but if no one's looking you can peek through the doorway. Covering the walls are carvings of scenes from Ramesses' military victories. From the first hall, eight statues of Osiris lead to a hypostyle hall. Beyond this second hall, deep in the heart of the temple, lies the sanctuary, with seated statues of Ramesses, and the gods Amun-Re, Re-Harakhte and Ptah.

Each vast statue of Osiris is a pillar 10m (32ft) high. Four statues stand on either side of the hallway.

All eight statues have Ramesses' face.

The door at the end leads to the sanctuary.

TOP TIPS FOR TOURISTS

No. 16: Re's rays

If you're here in October or February, try to visit the temple on the 20th. (You'll have to get up early, but it's worth it.) On those two days, just after dawn, the sun shines through the entrance and down the temple's entire length. For five minutes, the sanctuary statues at the far end are flooded with light.

ABU SIMBEL & NUBIA

QUEEN NEFERTARI'S TEMPLE

Beside the main temple is a smaller, simpler one, dedicated to Nefertari and the goddess Hathor.

That Ramesses should build a temple to one of his wives, even a chief one, is rare in itself. But statues of Nefertari also adorn the entrance, a privilege usually reserved for the king alone. It's certainly a more lasting token of affection than roses.

Remarkably, the statues of Nefertari are the same height as the four of husband Ramesses alongside.

45

SHOPPING

There are no shops as such, but every town or village you stop in will have a market. The choice of goods will depend on the size of the town and skills of its inhabitants. One town may have a good basket-maker, for instance, happy to trade a basket for a few beads. For top quality items, though, your best bet is a royal or temple workshop. Not surprisingly, the pharaoh keeps the best craftsmen for himself.

A typical market scene

Fruit, vegetables, bread and beer can be picked up daily.

Some craftsmen work from home, selling the finished products from their front yards.

SOUVENIRS

There's no shortage of unusual presents to take home. You could buy a pair of papyrus sandals to use as slippers. Mass-produced items include amulets and scarabs. Other easily portable items include cosmetics. At the other end of the scale, you could take back an inlaid wooden chest. An entire industry produces goods for the tomb, which anyone can buy. A shabti, complete with case, is an excellent souvenir.

FAÏENCE

Faïence (a type of glazed pottery) is used for everything from beads and vases to wall tiles. It's made by heating powdered quartz and always used to be bright blue. This is still its most common form, but faïence objects now also come in shades of yellow, red and green.

A faïence hedgehog – hedgehogs are thought to have magical powers of protection.

TOP TIPS FOR TOURISTS

No. 17: Cover ups

Examine expensive items marked as "ebony" very carefully. They may be made of cheap wood, which has simply been coated in thick black varnish. Be wary of painted items too. Paint is sometimes used to disguise a patchwork job, where several different woods have been used in one piece.

GLASSWARE

Glass-making is a relatively recent invention and you'll find amazingly decorated vases and dishes. Stripes are a common theme, made by winding threads of glass around a dish or vase and heating them until they merge in.

This open-mouthed glass fish is a container for perfumed oil.

POTTERY & STONE

Pots are made of clay and finely chopped straw, mixed by being trampled underfoot. Potters have wheels, but they are operated by hand. If the potter has no assistant to turn the wheel, he has to make his pots one-handed. The pots are then baked in a wood-burning kiln.

Recently, there's been a craze for painted pots. Stone is also used for pots and vases: limestone for household goods; alabaster for luxury items.

A gold, lion's-head necklace from the expensive end of the market

COSTUME JEWELS

Everyone here wears jewels to liven up an otherwise basic wardrobe. The choice ranges from a simple "lucky charm" necklace (three beads on a leather string), to an elaborate neck collar strung with thousands of beads.

If you're short of things to barter, go for less expensive copper items. But if money's no object, the gold and silver trinkets on offer will astound you. Stone beads also make necklaces pricey, as they're drilled by hand (which takes time). Cheaper by far are faïence beads.

ENTERTAINMENT

When it comes to entertainment, don't expect it laid out on a plate. There are no plays in Egypt, unless you count the performances put on by temples, dramatizing the lives of the gods. In fact, the only public spectacles (though well worth seeing) are religious festivals and royal processions. So, on the whole, people tend to make their own fun.

A pair of clappers used like castanets

PARTIES

All Egyptians love parties and the wealthy entertain on a grand scale. If you're invited to a banquet, it will be lavish. The food and drink will flow all night and you'll be entertained by jugglers, dancers, acrobats, wrestlers and storytellers. You won't need to lift a finger either. Servants bring all the refreshments to you.

66 I have heard that you have abandoned writing and that you whirl around in pleasures... 99

Teacher to a partying pupil

MUSIC

You'll hear a wide range of instruments (not to mention musicians). The oldest instrument is the reed or wooden flute, but bands also have oboes, lutes, or lyres, with drums and clappers (shown left) for rhythm. As the evening wears on, a harpist may accompany a storyteller.

DANCING

Even if the music has a lively beat, dancing is strictly a spectator sport. Routines are performed by professionals only. If you want to dance, you'll have to visit one of the seedier taverns. Here you can dance to your heart's content – but you'll take your life in your hands. You also risk arrest. Taverns are rowdy and frequently raided by the police.

A party in full swing

Only married couples sit together. For the single, it's girls with girls and boys with boys.

Your hosts will sit on chairs, but most guests sit on stools or cushions.

Dancing girls performing a well-rehearsed routine

Guests wear cones of perfumed fat on their heads. These melt during the evening, leaving everyone greasy but sweet-smelling.

TOYS & GAMES

Pulling the lever in the stomach of this wooden toy dog makes its mouth open.

Children grow up quickly, learning adult responsibilities from an early age. Toys, like the wooden dog above, painted dolls and balls, are soon left behind. Games, however, continue into adulthood, with board games called *Senet* and *Hounds and Jackals* being especially popular.

TOP TIPS FOR TOURISTS

No. 18: A quick dip

There are no swimming pools, but the Nile is clean to swim in. A word of warning: if you try it, look out for crocodiles.

SPORTS

Hunting and fishing are enjoyed by all sections of male society. Other sports, also for men only, include archery, wrestling, boxing and fencing with sticks. Men also enjoy swimming, as do women. (It's one of the few sports they can take part in.)

RIVER OUTINGS

Outside the home, most fun is to be had on the river. You can take out a boat, picnic on the river bank, or watch a boating contest. In a typical match, two teams, standing up in boats, try to knock each other into the river using long wooden poles.

Servants bring around water bowls, so you can rinse your fingers after the stickier courses.

A harpist and lute player accompany the dancers.

Faïence dishes piled high with dates for guests with a sweet tooth

Chatting about a forthcoming trip on the Nile

49

HUNTING & WILDLIFE

The Egyptians have two distinct views on nature. On the one hand, they certainly appreciate its beauty. You only have to study their paintings to see that. But they're also practical, convinced that nature exists for their personal use, whether food or sport. Don't feel you have to adopt local customs. You can enjoy the wildlife in its natural habitat without harming a hair.

HUNTING

Hunting is enjoyed by noblemen the world over and pharaohs are no exception. In the desert, Ramesses and his nobles trap lions or antelopes in nets, then let fly with arrows from the safety of their chariots. Huntsmen and dogs drive the animals into position beforehand, so it's not so much hunting as target practice.

A bull trapped in a makeshift pen

TOP TIPS FOR TOURISTS

No. 19: Watch out!

If you go on a desert hunt, be careful not to get in the way of the nobles in their chariots. Horses and chariots are very expensive. Any noble will put his team and chariot's safety above yours.

FOWLING

Fowling, or catching birds, is a living for peasants, who trap marsh birds in vast nets. Nobles, with the leisure to miss, toss a *throw-stick* (a curved piece of wood) at birds individually, hoping to break their necks.

If you hurl a throw-stick into a papyrus thicket, watch your aim. The first throw tells the birds you're there and they'll fly.

These two hunters aren't so much brave as foolhardy. Hunting a hippo usually takes a team of men.

A HIPPO HUNT

Lurking in the Nile are hippos and crocodiles and both are targeted by huntsmen. A hippo surfacing under a reed boat is certain disaster. But hippos aren't only killed because of the nuisance factor. A hippo hunt is dangerous – the ideal way for men to show off their courage and skill. There's also a religious side. The hippo is one of the forms taken by the evil god Set. The king is often shown harpooning a hippo, to symbolize the destruction of evil.

A model hippo made of faïence

FISHING

You'll meet two types of fishermen on the river. Nobles hunt for fun, fishing with baited hooks or using harpoons to spear fish as they swim by. Peasants, who fish to earn their living, work in teams and drag a net between two boats.

PETS

The Egyptians don't just think of animals as food or sport. Dogs are very popular as pets, short-legged lap dogs especially. Cats are now common too, though they were only adopted as pets in the Middle Kingdom. Other pets are monkeys, geese, and even gazelles.

Ramesses has a pet lion, "Tearer to pieces of his enemies", who roars into action alongside his chariot in war. You may spot "Tearer" in a procession, trotting beside the king. Ramesses also has a soft spot for two horses that saved his life in battle.

66 [It's] a happy day when we go down to the marsh... [to] ...snare birds and catch many fishes in the... waters. 99

Taken from "The Pleasures of Fishing and Fowling", an early manuscript

Fowling and fishing on the Nile

These days, only hunters use reed boats such as those shown here. Most other boats are made of wood.

A team of peasants checking the day's catch

Harpooning a fish rather than using a net needs quick reflexes.

51

FARMING

CROPS

Considering the vast amounts of bread and beer Egyptians consume, it's no surprise that the main crops are wheat (a type

Leeks, onions, garlic and peas

called emmer) and barley. Other crops grown include a wide variety of fruit and vegetables.

Some farmers grow flax, too, which is made into linen and used for clothes. Young flax plants make

Pomegranate, grapes and figs

fine thread; older ones provide a thicker thread, for heavy fabric, ropes and matting.

WINE PRODUCTION

Grapes are eaten off the vine and also used for wine. They're hand-picked, pressed twice to extract the juice, left in open jars to ferment, then poured into new jars and sealed.

Grapes are crushed by foot in a grape press. The juice is collected in a large tub or vat.

TILLING & SOWING

Wooden frames with bronze blades attached are used to till (turn over) the land before crops are sown. If the earth is too hard for lightweight blades, a hoe is used first. (Spades and shovels are unheard of.) Whatever the crop, animals are driven behind the sower, to ensure the seeds are well trodden in.

Tilling and sowing often take place together.

WATERING THE LAND

Since there's no rain, a network of canals was built centuries ago to store floodwater. The canals carry the water from the Nile to the fields via a series of connecting channels and ditches.

By alternately blocking and reopening channels, farmers can control the flow of water to their crops. To get the water from ditch to field, however, needs a strong fieldworker. A recent invention, the *shaduf* (shown below, to the left), makes life easier.

A shaduf is a bucket fixed to a counterweight and balanced on a beam. It may not seem hi-tech to you, but try lifting the bucket without it.

THE TAXMAN COMETH

Though everyone wants a good crop, it heralds the arrival of an unwelcome visitor: the taxman. Along with a team of civil servants, the taxman measures the growing crops, to assess how much will be harvested – and how much the pharaoh can cream off in taxes. A smart farmer has "gifts" on hand to help the taxman make this decision.

A taxman and civil servant measuring the crops while the farmer and his wife look on

Having to pay a percentage of his profit to the king, a farmer accepts with a resigned shrug. The problem arises when, whatever his eventual harvest, the original assessment stands. Even if a sudden plague of locusts wipes out an entire crop, the pharaoh can demand the same taxes as if the abundant crop forecast had materialized.

THE HARVEST

Probably, your only contact with the harvest, which falls in March and April, will be the easiest part of all: one of the numerous festivals to celebrate its end. For farmers, this is the culmination of several months of backbreaking work. The harvest itself has three stages:

Cutting: First, men cut the ears of grain with sickles. The grain is then carried away in baskets slung on poles or donkeys. Any left behind is gleaned (picked up) by women and children following close on the harvesters' heels.

Threshing: This is the second stage, where the grain is separated from the chaff (husks). The grain is scattered upon an area known as the threshing floor and roughly forked over, before cattle are let loose to trample upon it.

Winnowing: Finally, the flattened ears are scooped up by female workers and tossed into the air, a process called winnowing. The light chaff floats away, leaving the grain. This is stored in granaries, the amount carefully recorded by a scribe before the king's cut is carted off.

If you visit at harvest time, you'll see winnowing women.

ANNUAL CYCLE

Once all is safely gathered in, irrigation ditches must be repaired and new channels dug, ready for the floods in July. After that, farming halts until October, when farmers repair any flood damage and check that the boundary stones marking their fields are still in place.

RELIGION & FESTIVALS

RELIGION

For Egyptians, religion is so bound up with everyday life it's inseparable from it. Gods aren't remote deities. They live among them – if only in spirit form – hidden in temples.

Egyptian beliefs arose as an attempt to explain the mysteries of the world, though explanations can vary, depending on where in Egypt you are. To make things more complicated, over the last 2,000 years, as new beliefs have developed, old ideas have simply been tagged on to them.

One of the most common themes is the balance of order against chaos. This "order" is maintained by temple rituals, living a decent life and the king ruling with justice.

THE PEOPLE'S RELIGION

Since few people may go beyond temple courtyards (and most can't get that far), small shrines have been set up where locals can pray to the gods and leave offerings. Rooms in Egyptian homes have niches where statues of gods are kept. Many people also carry amulets with charms to ward off evil spirits. It's at this point religion and magic become blurred. The Egyptians are strong believers in the power contained in objects. Don't offend anyone or they may attack an effigy (model) of you.

The theories of creation

Re created all things. One theory says he emerged from a sacred lotus flower.

Some say Re was hatched from an egg laid by the Great Cackler, a goose.

Others think Re first appeared as a scarab beetle.

TEMPLES & PRIESTS

There's no organized religion as such. Temples aren't places of worship; they're where the gods live. Priests don't preach; they are live-in servants, feeding and entertaining the gods three times a day. Egyptians feel an overwhelming gratitude for all the gods have given them. It's only fair, runs the argument, that the gods get the best of everything in return. Any food the gods don't eat is passed on to temple workers as wages. Temples are the largest employers in Egypt. Karnak alone has over 81,000 on the payroll.

PURE IN BODY

To an Egyptian, cleanliness isn't next to godliness, it *is* godliness. Demons are said to live in dirt and priests wash seven times and chew natron (a salt) to cleanse themselves, every time they enter a temple. They only wear white linen, which is frequently washed. On top of that, they shave all over every other day.

Near a temple, don't be surprised if someone wafts an incense burner up your tunic. He's simply trying to smoke out demons.

FESTIVALS

Festivals are a chance for Egyptians to interact more closely with their gods, since on these occasions the statues are brought out from the shrines. The first one described below ensures the well-being of the king. If he stays well, says the theory, so will Egypt.

Sed (Jubilee): an ancient custom, celebrated on the 30th anniversary of a king's reign and periodically after that. The king runs between two markers to prove his fitness to rule and renew his strength.

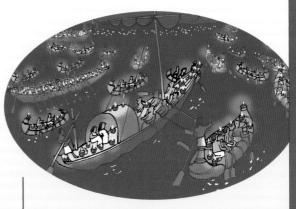

Boats cross the Nile in the early morning for the Feast of the Valley. The Nile is ablaze with candles and torches.

The king running for Sed: today the run is symbolic.

Opet: a more recent festival, held at the start of the year. The barques (sacred boats) of the god Amun, his wife Mut and son Khonsu are carried in procession from the temple at Karnak to Luxor, about 3km (almost a couple of miles) away.

Feast of the Valley: this may be a festival for the dead but it's a lively affair. The statue of Amun is taken from its shrine at Karnak and ferried over to the tombs on the West Bank.

If you don't mind heights, arrive early and climb the West Bank cliffs. There's a competition to see who can be the first to spot the glint of gold that indicates Amun's statue has left the temple. Tombs are lit by lamplight and families hold banquets for their dead relatives.

Mystery Plays: for a little drama, visit Abydos to see a masked play about Osiris and Set (see page 32). You could join in but be prepared for it to degenerate into a brawl. Religion is taken seriously over here. Egyptians support their chosen gods with all the enthusiasm of football fans.

Priests acting out a mystery play

CLOTHES & FASHION

WHAT'S HOT

Little changed in fashion for 1,500 years. What was worn in the First Dynasty was still trendy throughout the Middle Kingdom. But, as the New Kingdom continues, suddenly fashion itself is all the rage. Clothes are looser, more flowing and far more elaborate, and pleats are very much in.

Noblemen wear a kilt (wraparound skirt) topped by layers of fine pleated robes tied at the waist with a sash. Upper class women wear fine dresses, topped with a shawl made from one piece of cloth.

A loose, thin cloak for men is very fashionable.

Dresses and tunics for the lower classes are simpler and made from coarser cloth. Linen is the main fabric (often white, as that's thought pure) and used for almost everything – although winter wraps and cloaks are sometimes made from wool.

Noblewomen's shawls are folded around the body and knotted on the chest.

WHAT'S NOT

Until recently, most men wore only a short linen kilt. Women had an equally simple sheath dress to the ankles, held up by shoulder straps. Children wore kilts too, though in summer they usually ran around naked. Officials and noblemen wore longer, pleated kilts, while noblewomen's dresses were patterned and dyed different shades.

An elaborate Middle Kingdom party frock, covered with beads.

HAIR & WIGS

Most people shave their heads to keep cool and then wear a fancy wig made from human or artificial hair. During the Middle Kingdom, padded and decorated hair was in vogue for a while. Men now keep their hair shortish. The trend for women was long and straight, but masses of braids and curls are now in. Children have shaved heads (to prevent lice) but keep enough hair for a braid: "the sidelock of youth". In paintings, a subject shown with no clothes and a shaved head is a child.

Woman

New Kingdom hairstyles à la mode

Man

A boy's sidelock (girls' braids are longer)

SHOES

Everyone goes barefoot for much of the time. For occasions when you need to be more formal, slip on sandals made from papyrus reeds or leather. The upper classes tend to go in for highly decorated footwear. Tutankhamun had a snazzy pair of gold embossed sandals for special occasions.

Papyrus sandals are ideal footwear for the climate.

Mirrors have faces of polished silver, as here, or copper. Glass isn't used.

Kohl, made from lead or copper mixed with oil, comes in black or green. Paint it liberally around your eyes to keep flies away. Red ochre (clay) is used to redden cheeks and lips but boys may want to leave that to the girls. Don't worry if plastering on cosmetics is bad for your skin. You'll even find preparations to cure acne.

TOILETRIES

It's not just priests who keep clean. Everyone washes, either in the river or with a jug and basin, if not a shower, at home. There's no soap, but you'll find a cleansing cream made from oil, lime and perfume readily available. As for shampoo – there are mixtures to cure dandruff and baldness. Tempted to change your hair shade? You can buy henna shampoo and dye your hair red.

COSMETICS

Both sexes wear cosmetics and perfumed oils, partly as a fashion statement but mostly as protection against the fierce Egyptian sun. You should rub in oils daily to prevent your skin from cracking and drying out. Stock up on kohl eye paint too.

A box for eye paint

ACCESSORIES

Jewels are worn by everyone from the pharaoh to the poorest peasant, to decorate fairly basic clothing. If bracelets and rings aren't your thing, try a pectoral (fancy pendant hung around the neck) or an ever-popular bead collar. Important men also carry a staff to show off their social standing.

A pectoral and the latest fashion item: big earrings

EDUCATION

THE WRITE THING

When you consider that the majority of the population can't read and write, it's hardly surprising that those who can are highly thought of. Scribes, who write and copy texts and keep records, enjoy great privileges, prestige and power. For some, it's the first step up the ladder of government service.

A statue of a scribe

SCHOOL OF KNOCKS

Children are taught by scribes, who aren't necessarily good teachers. Many believe, "a boy's ears are on his back." In other words, to get him to listen, beat him. Insults, such as, "You... are thicker than a tall obelisk..." are par for the course. No one's beaten for talking though. Even scribes read words aloud before they copy them down.

SCHOOLS

Public schools, attached to temples, government offices and the palace, are for the sons of scribes and the higher classes only. Most boys from poorer families learn their fathers' trades; girls help their mothers at home. A few villages have schools run by local priests or scribes, though they charge. Even so, many peasants struggle to scrape the fees together. Some nobles prefer to educate their sons at home, hiring a private tutor. Daughters are often included in these lessons.

LESSONS

Boys start their first school at seven. Perhaps because scribes are not formally trained as teachers, lessons are uninspired. There's no alphabet, so pupils spend hours memorizing characters and phrases for the Egyptian scripts (see pages 60-61).

The rest of the day is spent learning parrot-fashion, or copying classic works, such as *The Wisdom Texts* which lay down rules for how to behave. It's hoped that boys will absorb the advice while copying.

Egyptian boys from noble families writing down an ancient story their teacher is dictating

SECONDARY SCHOOL

Pupils go on to higher education at nine or ten. At this stage, they learn how to compose letters and legal documents, studying a range of subjects. Along with geography, history, languages and literature, religion and mathematics, boys are taught engineering, surveying, account-keeping, astronomy and medicine.

An astronomer's star chart showing the constellations in the form of gods

Students from wealthy families then specialize in only one or two subjects, such as engineering or languages, and enter government service. But most of the students go on to become scribes of some sort.

WRITING KIT

Young boys write on pieces of pottery or limestone flakes (known as *ostraka*), or wooden tablets covered with plaster.

A piece of ostrakon* which tells a popular tale

The tablets can be washed and used again, in much the same way as a blackboard.

*Ostrakon is the singular of ostraka

PEN AND PAPER

Once they can write fluently, boys move on to writing on sheets of papyrus, a paper made from papyrus reeds. They write using reed pens and black, red or green ink made from mineral pigments. Ink comes in solid blocks and has to be mixed with water on a palette before it can be used, like paint.

Papyrus is the closest thing the Egyptians have to paper. Bear in mind that it varies in quality. If you're thinking of buying any, the best comes from the middle of the papyrus pith. It goes through several stages before you can write on it. Even then, it feels more like fabric than paper.

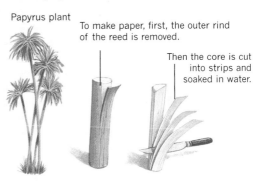

Papyrus plant
To make paper, first, the outer rind of the reed is removed.
Then the core is cut into strips and soaked in water.

Two layers of strips are pressed together at right angles. Starch in the core acts like glue. The sheet is beaten with a mallet and left to dry.

Finally, it is polished with a stone. Lots of sheets are joined together to form a scroll.

WRITE LIKE AN EGYPTIAN

HIEROGLYPHS

The Egyptians write using symbols known as *hieroglyphs*. As there are over 700 of them, you're unlikely to learn them all on one visit. You may start to recognize the more common ones, though, and you can always use this page as a handy reference.

Hieroglyphs take the form of pictures, but they're not simply picture writing. Originally, they just stood for the object they show but now they stand for sounds too.

A picture of an owl stands for the sound of an "m".

Words are made up of several different symbols. An extra picture, called a determinative, is often placed at the end of a word, so there's no doubt about its meaning.

For example:

The sounds of "m", "j" and "w" make up the word "cat" but the sign has a cat on the end, too, to make it clear.

m   j   w

The hieroglyphs above are in an oval frame called a cartouche. They show the name Tutankhamun took on becoming king: Neb-kheperu-re.

NO A, E, I, O, U...

There are no hieroglyphs for vowels. (It's only in the 19th century AD, when texts are translated, that scholars will give vowel sounds to some symbols, to make them easier to read.) The Egyptians don't worry about spelling either. They're far more concerned that a word looks right.

The word for beautiful, "nfr", is not written in a line, as above, but to fit a neat rectangle:

THE POWER OF THE PEN

"Hieroglyph" is a Greek word meaning "holy writing" but the Egyptians think of hieroglyphs as the "words of the gods".

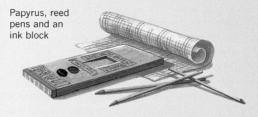

Papyrus, reed pens and an ink block

They believe words have magical powers, creating the objects they describe – which is why hieroglyphs cover their temples and tombs.

READING ORDER

Hieroglyphs can be read from right to left, left to right or straight down. The way they're set out gives you the clue. If the people and animals in the pictures are facing left, you start from the left. If they face right, you read from right to left.

Read from left to right

Read from right to left

This column of hieroglyphs should be read from right to left and down.

Hieroglyphs you read down are often used on pillars or columns. Look out for them on the temples at Thebes.

Pharaohs' names are easy to spot as they are always shown in cartouches.

SHORTHAND

Hieroglyphs are always used on monuments but, for everyday use, two shorthand scripts called "Hieratic" and "Demotic" have been developed. These simplify the pictures and look more like handwriting.

Hieratic   **Demotic**

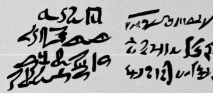

AN ALPHABET

a = (vulture)
b = (leg)
d = (hand)
i = (reed)
f = (viper)
g = (stand for a jar)
k = (a slope)
r = (mouth)
s = (folded cloth)
t = (loaf of bread)
h = (house with courtyard)
j = (cobra)
k = (basket)
m = (owl)
n = (water)
p = (wicker stool)
w = (quail)
y = (double reed)
s = (door bolt)

This is just to give an idea of which hieroglyphs match letters in a modern alphabet.

GOVERNMENT & LAW

A PYRAMID SOCIETY

At the top of society is the pharaoh, the absolute ruler. Despite having absolute power, the pharaoh has no easy life (though admittedly, he has it easier than most). The king is expected to maintain the balance of the entire universe. He's responsible for the weather and harvest. He's a go-between for the gods and his people, and if Egypt goes to war, he must lead the army into battle.

Though the pharaoh has the final say, the day-to-day running of Egypt is in the hands of government departments. These include the Treasury, Royal Works (temples and tombs), the Granaries, Cattle and Foreign Affairs.

After the pharaoh, the two most important men are the viziers, one each in charge of Upper and Lower Egypt.

A pyramid of people showing the structure of Egyptian society

GOING DOWN

Below government officers, high priests and scribes, mayors and governors run town and country districts. All have a staff of officials to collect taxes and carry out the orders of government departments. Lower down the pyramid come soldiers, craftsmen and farmers, followed by peasants and servants, with slaves at the bottom of the lot.

CLASS SNOBBERY

Even within classes, there's a definite order. Take scribes, for example. At the lowest level are clerks and letter-writers. One step up are community scribes and business secretaries. Nearer the top are local or regional officials, or scribes who administer an estate or temple. At the very top are the highest-ranking government officials.

Pharaoh

Viziers

Government ministers and high priests

Scribes belonging to many ranks

Town mayors, district governors, priests and doctors

Soldiers

Craftsmen

Farmers and townspeople

Peasants

Slaves

TAXES

There are numerous taxes, paid with either produce or work. You should escape these though. There's no tax on tourists. Among the taxes are:
Tributes from conquered people in places such as Syria,
Land tax paid by farmers in grain, based on an estimated crop,
Craft tax paid by craftsmen on the goods they produce,
Hunting and fishing tax paid on all fish and game sold,
Import/export tax paid by traders.

A glass-blower might pay his taxes in jugs

CORVÉE DUTY

Corvée is a tax paid for in work and everyone but the ruling classes is forced to undertake it. Officially, no one is exempt. In practice, the rich often pay poorer citizens to do their corvée for them. Corvée helps to ensure that vital jobs, such as irrigation repairs, are carried out. When the ground is too flooded to work on, farmers are sent to help out on the latest building project or down a quarry or mine.

WOMEN IN EGYPT

Women have a better time of it in Egypt than in many ancient cultures, with much personal freedom and the same legal duties and rights as men. A wife keeps her own property after divorce and a girl may inherit her father's estate – though this is more likely if she has no brothers.

JOBS FOR THE GIRLS

Though they are expected to marry young and raise a family, some women have a career outside the home. They can run businesses or farms (paying taxes), or become maids to noblewomen, gaining influence in important households. Temples take on female dancers, musicians and singers, and noblewomen can become courtiers or priestesses. Jobs for lower class girls include weaving, perfume-making and professional mourning.

Any girl can become a dancer – if she's fit enough. Some of the routines are very demanding.

LAW AND ORDER

There are laws on every aspect of life, upheld by the Medjay and, in a dispute, a *kenbet* (town court). All Egyptians, however poor, can have their day in court, as they represent themselves. They're always suing each other, so you may be called as a witness. Judges are local officials, who have been known to seek signs from the gods if they can't decide on a verdict. In criminal cases, the accused is innocent until proven guilty, but anyone found guilty is suitably punished.

THE PASSING OF TIME

THE SEASONS

With farming the main way of life for most Egyptians, it makes sense for the seasons to be based around the farming year. There are three:

Inundation (Akhet): from July to October, this is the annual flooding of the Nile, without which all of Egypt would be a barren desert.

Planting (Proyet): from November to February, when everyone gets out in the fields to sow and tend crops.

Summer (Shemu): from March to June, when the crops are harvested.

DAYS & HOURS

Not only will you find no watches, both the calendar and the Egyptian method of telling the time are arbitrary affairs.

Calendars: Though the Egyptians have three calendars, none is that accurate. The first – the farming calendar – is based around the flooding of the Nile. Twelve months of thirty days each now make up a 360-day year. Since this is five days' short, five holy days (festivals) have been stuck on the end, ensuring that the old year goes out with a bang. There are ten days in a week and every tenth day is a holiday.

But, since the Egyptians have no leap years, this calendar gains a day with every four years. After a few centuries, "Inundation" on the calendar and the actual flooding of the Nile are way off.

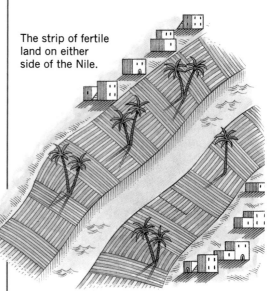

The strip of fertile land on either side of the Nile.

Irrigation canals run from the Nile to water the fields.

So, a second calendar, based on the stars, has been introduced to help. This is thanks to sharp-eyed astronomers, who saw that the star Sirius always rose with the sun around the time of Inundation.

The third calendar, a lunar one, is based around the phases of the moon. It's used by priests to regulate rituals and festivals. You'll often see a moon calender of festivals inscribed on a temple wall.

A useful point to remember is that years themselves are only numbered from the start of a king's reign. So, when Ramesses II took the throne, the calendar went back to Year 1.

Time, based around a 24-hour day, is measured using water clocks. Water drains out of a pot which has been divided into hour-long sections and marked off.

ANCIENT GREECE

ABOUT GREECE

Greece, its beaches lapped by the sparkling Mediterranean Sea, is an idyllic destination. Spiny mountain ranges run down the length of the country, but the jagged coastline has dozens of inlets, making it easy to travel around by boat. And, as the mainland is surrounded by hundreds of islands, you've a good chance to get in some island-hopping.

This section begins with a quick run-down on Ancient Greece through the ages. If you're not in the least bothered about how it got to where it is now, and just want to see it in all its glory, check out the page opposite for some useful tips before you dive in.

IN THE BEGINNING

1. Almost 40,000 years ago and people were already around.

2. Civilization arrives some time later. By 2000BC, the Minoans are living it up on Crete. But that lasts barely a millennium (1,000 years).

3. 1600BC and it's the turn of a people called the Mycenaeans to dominate mainland Greece.

4. But, only 400 years later, they're destroyed by war and famine.

THEN

5. The Dark Ages hit, not for the Greeks but for us (because we're in the dark about what was going on).

6. After 300 years of darkness, the "Archaic Period" begins: people write and paint again – leaving us masses of useful evidence about their lives – and travel becomes popular.

7. The country is divided into independent city-states (each one known as a *polis*), ruled by aristocrats or sometimes one man, called a "tyrant".

NOW

8. The "Classical Period" dawns and it's a Golden Age. It only lasts from 500-336BC, so time your visit to make the most of it.

9. The city of Athens grows to dominate all the other city-states. Between 479-431BC, everyone who's anyone visits Athens. Ready to join them?

Pericles, current ruler of Athens

CURRENCY

You can pick up currency on arrival, but be sure to bring a good supply of spices from home. You'll need to trade them for your first batch of coins. Many places also accept spices instead of cash. Coins, usually silver, are decorated with Greek heroes or animals and you're most likely to use *drachmas* and *obols* (1/6 drachma). The only minor annoyance is that each city-state issues its own coins.*

A WORD OF WARNING!

Watch what company you keep. Get in with a rowdy crowd and you'll not only get a bad reputation, you'll risk being deported.

ALPHABET SOUP

Although the Ancient Greeks have their own – distinctive – alphabet, many letters may be familiar. The alphabet was adapted from one used by the Phoenicians (traders from the eastern Mediterranean), and will form the template for all modern European ones. Below is a list of the Ancient Greek letters and their modern equivalents:

Αα	A	Ηη	E	Νν	N	Ττ	T
Ββ	B	Θθ	th	Ξξ	X	Υυ	U
Γγ	G	Ιι	I	Οο	O	Φφ	ph
Δδ	D	Κκ	K	Ππ	P	Χχ	ch
Εε	E	Λλ	L	Ρρ	R	Ψψ	ps
Ζζ	Z	Μμ	M	Σσ	S	Ωω	O

* See page 92 for how to change money

SEASIDE SCARES

Sprawling on a beach or splashing around in the sea are great ways to unwind during a culture-loaded break. But be careful! Two of the greatest risks to tourists are sunburn and poisonous sea creatures.

To protect against sunburn, keep covered up or pack cream from home. Girls shouldn't be sunbathing in their new bikinis anyway, unless they've found a very secluded cove.

Sea creatures to avoid include jellyfish and sea urchins, though this is easier said than done. Pack baking soda – good for jellyfish stings* – and a small sewing kit. If you sterilize the needle over a flame, you can use it to remove the stings of sea urchins.

TOP TIPS FOR TOURISTS

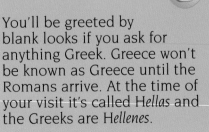

No. 2: It's all Greek to me

You'll be greeted by blank looks if you ask for anything Greek. Greece won't be known as Greece until the Romans arrive. At the time of your visit it's called *Hellas* and the Greeks are *Hellenes*.

---

* US = "stingers"

67

ATHENS & THE ACROPOLIS

If you're like most visitors, you'll make **Athens** your first stop. With the recent boom in art and trade, it's a very good place to start. The city is dominated by the **Acropolis** (its name means "high city"), the rocky hill where the Athenians first settled.

As the city expanded, houses and shops were built around the base of the hill. The Acropolis was left as you'll see it today, a sanctuary for temples and shrines.

To help you get your bearings, the picture below shows the layout of the city. The smaller plan is to guide you around the Acropolis itself. Bear in mind, though, that if you come earlier than 437BC, not all of the temples are finished – or even there.

A view of the city of Athens, with the Acropolis in the distance

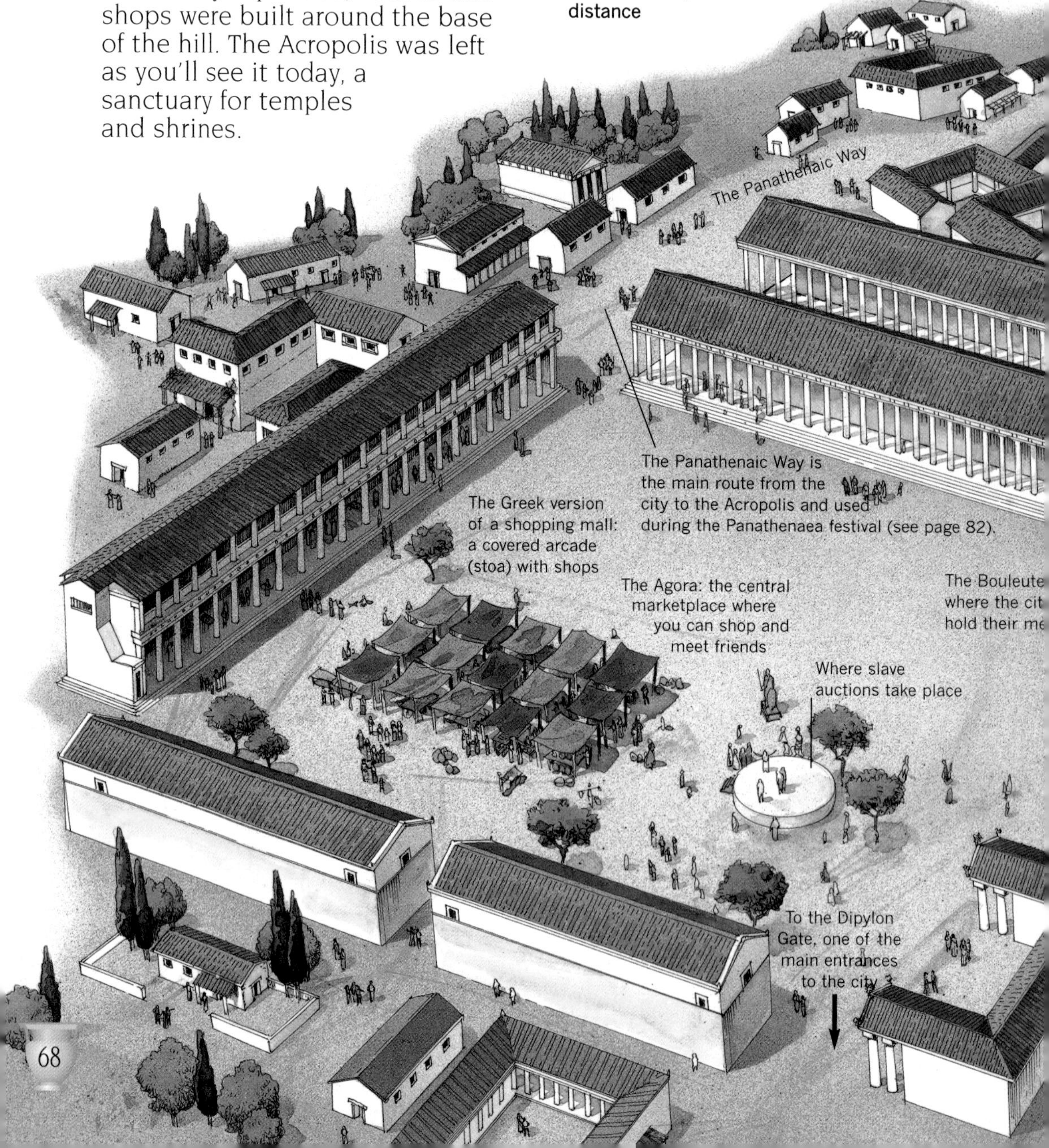

The Panathenaic Way

The Panathenaic Way is the main route from the city to the Acropolis and used during the Panathenaea festival (see page 82).

The Greek version of a shopping mall: a covered arcade (stoa) with shops

The Agora: the central marketplace where you can shop and meet friends

The Bouleute where the cit hold their me

Where slave auctions take place

To the Dipylon Gate, one of the main entrances to the city

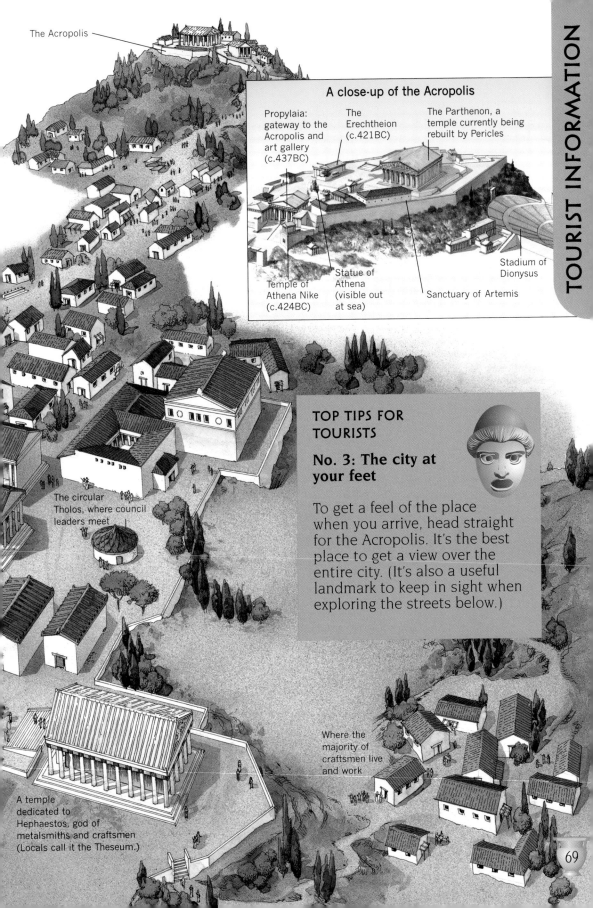

The Acropolis

A close-up of the Acropolis

Propylaia: gateway to the Acropolis and art gallery (c.437BC)

The Erechtheion (c.421BC)

The Parthenon, a temple currently being rebuilt by Pericles

Stadium of Dionysus

Temple of Athena Nike (c.424BC)

Statue of Athena (visible out at sea)

Sanctuary of Artemis

TOP TIPS FOR TOURISTS

No. 3: The city at your feet

To get a feel of the place when you arrive, head straight for the Acropolis. It's the best place to get a view over the entire city. (It's also a useful landmark to keep in sight when exploring the streets below.)

The circular Tholos, where council leaders meet

A temple dedicated to Hephaestos, god of metalsmiths and craftsmen (Locals call it the Theseum.)

Where the majority of craftsmen live and work

69

WHERE TO STAY

Most tourists stay with friends or relatives en route to their destination. But this isn't really an option for a time tourist (unless you speak fluent Ancient Greek and make friends quickly).

As the weather stays warm for most of the year, why not join the locals and camp out? In towns, people happily sleep under the porches of public buildings. There are no worries here of being moved along with the sarcastic comment, "Haven't you got a home to go to?"

Slaves' rooms

Bathr

Kitchen: slaving over a hot stove

Lifting the roof off: inside a Greek house

Altar

Lobby

A potter's workshop

A guard outside a hotel: hotels are very exclusive, largely catering for the very rich and famous.

HOTELS

The largest towns have hotels, called *katagogia*, and it's always worth trying to book into one, just for the experience. If they're not booked up – and you're persuasive – you may be able to talk your way in. On the whole, though, katagogia are reserved for VIPs. Humble tourists are shown the door.

HOME SWEET HOME

If camping isn't for you, you may be able to rent rooms in a private house. Think yourself lucky if you get to stay in a house the size of the one above. Most are much smaller, though with similar rooms. Many also have a central courtyard, with the rooms facing in. (People here have a thing about privacy.)

Since only larger houses have space to rent rooms, you can be sure of comfortable surroundings. There may even be a bakery on the ground floor, so you won't have far to walk for your bread. House rules are few, but remember: never go near the women's quarters without being invited. Trespass and you risk the wrath (and fists) of your landlord.

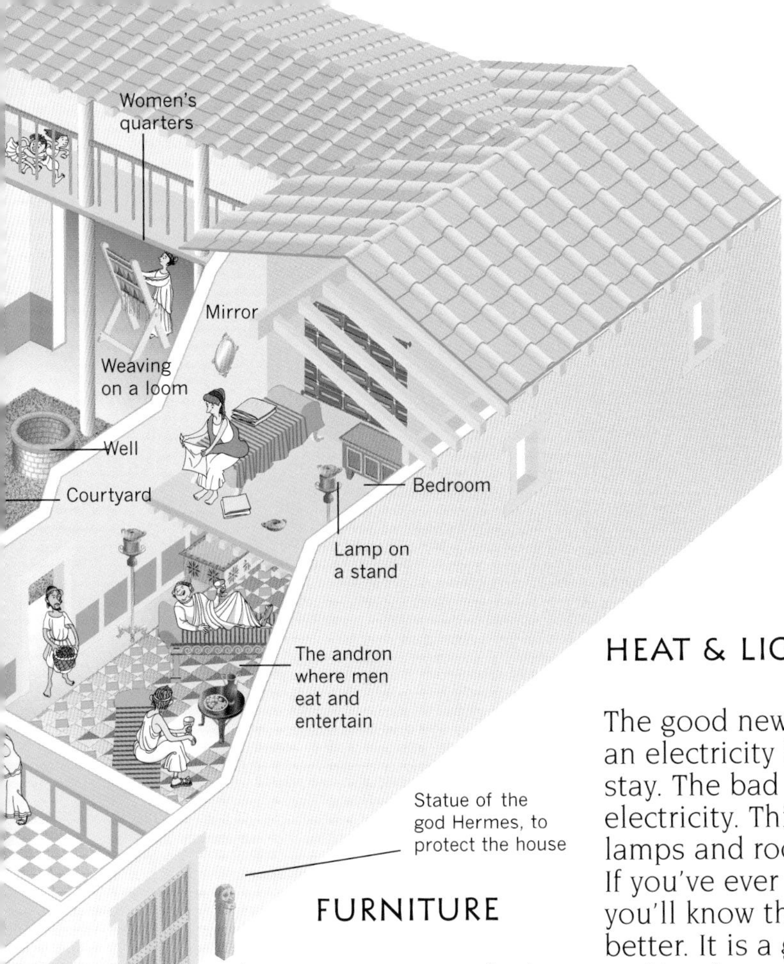

Women's quarters

Mirror

Weaving on a loom

Well

Courtyard

Bedroom

Lamp on a stand

The andron where men eat and entertain

Statue of the god Hermes, to protect the house

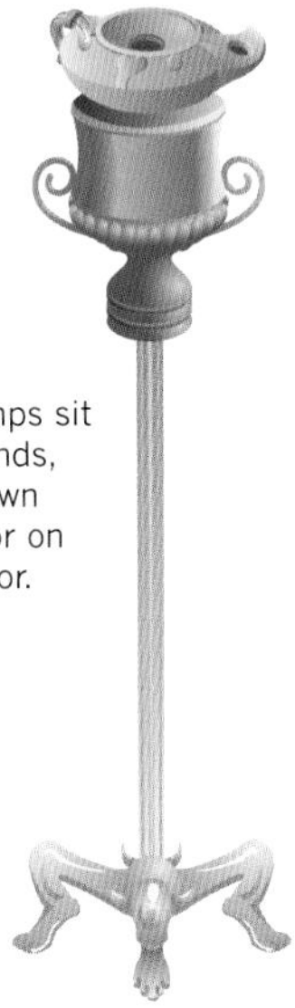

Oil lamps sit on stands, as shown here, or on the floor.

HEAT & LIGHT

The good news is you won't face an electricity bill at the end of your stay. The bad news? There's no electricity. This means relying on oil lamps and rooms aren't that well-lit. If you've ever read by candlelight, you'll know the more wicks the better. It is a gentler light though, making for cosy evenings. If you're cold, you could borrow a brazier (a metal container on a stand in which you burn charcoal).

FURNITURE

There's not a great deal of furniture and it's mostly wooden – elaborately carved and inlaid with ivory, silver and gold in wealthier households. The master of the house sits on a *thronos* (fancy chair); women have smaller chairs. You'll probably have to make do with a stool. But eating is done lying down (on couches), and tables are low, to slide under the couches when not in use. Beds have sheets, a mattress and pillows, so you should at least have a good night's sleep.

Thronos

Most tables are three-legged.

TOP TIPS FOR TOURISTS
No. 4: Burglar alarm!

Houses are built of wood and mud bricks which have been hardened in the sun. This makes their walls very easy to tunnel through – as many home owners know to their cost. So, when you go out, take your valuables with you. Better yet, don't bring them away with you in the first place.

71

WHAT TO EAT

Ancient Greece is an ideal destination for healthy eaters, not to mention vegetarians. Most people live on – "enjoy" isn't really the word – a diet of barley porridge. This is livened up with bread, cheese, eggs and plenty of fruit and vegetables.

If you can't live without meat, be sure to bring enough spices to trade with. Only the wealthy can eat meat every day. But for the rich, there's the usual choice of lamb, pork and poultry, plus goat. You'll even find beef – though there's very little grazing land to raise cows, which makes beef even more costly. You might want to wait until the end of the trip before blowing the last of your budget on that large steak.

TOP TIPS FOR TOURISTS

No. 5: Catch of the day

Whether dining out or self-catering, your best bet is to fill up on fish. The seas around the coast are brimming with different types, so there's plenty of variety and it's always freshly caught. Squid is particularly popular. It's also delicious (though if badly cooked can be more rubbery than an eraser).

THE MAIN MEAL

You may have heard the expression, "Breakfast like a king, dine like a pauper." Well, the Greeks live it in reverse. (Except for the poor, who eat like paupers all the time.) With breakfast simply a little bread soaked in wine and lunch a light snack, everyone builds up an appetite for dinner.

CHEERS!

The most common drink is wine, always diluted with water and mixed in a vast container, or *krater*. If that's not for you, quench your thirst at one of the many public fountains.

Kraters can be huge. Some are the size of a large dog.

OLIVES

Olives or their oil turn up in almost every Greek dish in some form or other. Olives are pressed several times over for the different grades of oil, which is used for medicine and fuel, as well as cooking. The best oil (the one used in cooking) comes from the first pressing.

An olive press

DINNER PARTIES

Luckily for the male tourist, the Greeks don't like eating alone, so invitations to dinner are frequent. You could also be taken along as a friend of a guest. Women and young children eat in a separate room, except at private family occasions.

Everyone reclines on cushions to eat and many diners bring their own. The most important guest is seated on the host's right. You can tell how popular you are by how close you're sitting to the host.

The courses are endless: fish, meat and vegetable dishes, cheeses, nuts and pastries. But food is incidental to the main business of the evening – drinking and the after-dinner discussion (see pages 78-79).

> " *In some parts they call a sumptuous banquet, "Having a bite to eat."* "
>
> **Socrates, a philosopher**

PARTY ETIQUETTE

Dress smartly and arrive on time. The other diners won't wait. Slaves will rinse and perfume your feet at the door. (If you've spent all day on foot, sightseeing, the slaves will be grateful if you've washed them first.)

They'll also bring water for you to rinse your hands. You'll mostly eat with your fingers, though there are spoons. But don't look for napkins. Instead, guests wipe their hands on a special paste. (Don't eat it by mistake!)

If you arrive late, the best seats may have gone.

You can enjoy live music while you eat.

Just wave a hand to have your cup refilled.

The food is brought in, already laid out on tables.

Male diners are entertained with the witty chat of professional female companions.

A dinner party getting under way

73

GETTING AROUND

Greece's spectacular mountains make for great views, but they're not such fun when it comes to getting around. The country's hilly terrain makes travel hard going, and most of the decent roads tend to lead to the religious sites. Fine if these are on your itinerary, but not much help if you're "templed" out.

Try to avoid war zones.

The busiest routes have reasonable roads. Rivers have few bridges, but water levels are low in the summer so this shouldn't be a problem. But you'll face long hold-ups if you travel in winter, as chariots and carts continually get stuck in mud.

Try to travel light: unless you can afford a mule to carry your backpack, you'll be lugging it on foot. If walking isn't for you, buy a horse and perhaps a carriage. You can always sell them on at the end of your stay. But you'll need plenty of money. Horses are expensive because there are so few places with enough pasture to feed them.

You won't get saddle-sore. There are no saddles.

Most people walk everywhere, often carrying a walking stick and folding stool. Don't laugh. Within a day, you'll follow their example. The stick helps on the rough ground and the stool is a godsend – there are no handy roadside coffee stops. Another vital accessory is a torch (of the flaming variety). With no street lighting whatsoever, you'll be relying on the moon and stars when darkness falls.

TRAVEL WARNING

Some parts of the country – the rockier highland routes in particular – are infested with bandits. If you plan to travel overland, try to band together with locals going the same way. The frequent wars between states make travel dangerous too.

Plan your route carefully before you set out, or you'll have to take long detours to avoid trouble spots. Sparta in particular is usually at war and you don't want to get caught up in a battle, or worse, arrested as a spy.

Bandits lie in wait for the footsore and travel-worn.

SEA TRAVEL

Wherever possible, make journeys by sea. Boats are the easiest and quickest way to travel and you're sure to find a merchant ship to take you – for a reasonable fee. Greece has hundreds of natural inlets and creeks, which means wherever you are you're close to the sea. Even heading inland, you can probably make most of the trip by boat.

An early anchor

The best time to sail is summer, though remember boats rely on wind power. Ironically, you'll face delays if the weather's too good and your ship is becalmed. There's also the threat of storms, the rocky coast and, worse still, pirates. Luckily, your visit coincides with a time when the Athenian navy is most powerful. With the seas carefully policed, pirate ships are at an all time low.

But be warned: pirates don't all sail under the Jolly Roger. It's not unknown for a crew to turn on their own passengers and rob them once they're out at sea. So, be careful whose ship you board. And make sure the captain offers a sacrifice to the sea god Poseidon before you set out. It can't hurt and shows he takes his responsibility seriously.

TOP TIPS FOR TOURISTS

No. 6: Travel inn

As you've probably already found, inns are few and far between. Luckily for the tourist, the Ancient Greeks have a custom of hospitality. In fact, it's more of a duty. If you need a place to stay, you can knock on almost any door and be sure of a welcome. But treat your hosts with respect and be sure to repay them handsomely, with gifts from home.

> **"** *...in order to defraud their creditors, they laid a plot to sink [the ship]* **"**

Demosthenes, a great orator
(with a useful reminder to be careful whose ship you travel on)

A merchant ship to avoid: its crew looks distinctly unfriendly

There are stories of hapless passengers being thrown overboard and rescued by dolphins – but you can't rely on them.

ANCIENT GREECE: MAIN SIGHTS

Lesbos

② **Kos** The island where Hippocrates has set up his medical school

The gold and ivory statue of Athene stands in her temple on the **Acropolis**.

they're not out causing trouble elsewhere

Selling fresh fish

THESSALY

⑤ **Delphi**
Home of the famous oracle, who can answer any question you care to ask

The Pythia (oracle at Delphi) having a vision

A trireme (Greek warship)

ATTICA

① **Athens** The city-state with everything, including an enormous statue of Athene

Piraeus Port of ③ Athens and home to traders from everywhere

⑨ **Delos** Island-hoppers should stop off here where the Delian League (an alliance of Greek states) met for the first time.

Unlike merchant ships, triremes have oars as well as sails.

⑦ **Laurion** Site of the ancient world's largest silver mines

Mediterranean Sea

Crete Island home of the fabled Minotaur

• Mycenae

• Argos

A Spartan warrior keeping his slave hard at it

④ **Olympia**   **ARCADIA**

See the original Olympics here.

MESSENIA

⑧ **Sparta** Home of the scary Spartans: for information only. <u>DON'T</u> visit!

PELOPONNESE

A merchant ship setting off to trade silver for silk and spices

IF YOU GET SICK...

You've come to the right place. Greek doctors have excellent reputations. They tend to fall into two camps – though these aren't mutually exclusive. Some, mainly priests, believe in the old ideas, swearing by Asclepius, the god of healing. But many others now follow Hippocrates, man of medicine.

PRIESTS & PRAYERS

Most families rely on herbal cures. If these fail, they call in a priest. In fact, sleeping in one of Asclepius' temples has been known to produce miraculous results. If not, the priests can offer home-made remedies of their own.

Visit a temple and you'll have to perform certain sacrifices before spending the night. You must also undergo a "purification" ceremony, probably involving vast amounts of holy water. Ideally, Asclepius should heal you as you sleep. Or, he may tell you via a dream the treatment you need. Of course, you may also wake up no better.

Dreaming a cure

A THANK-YOU GIFT

If Asclepius does help, you should leave him an offering – usually a model of the body part he's cured. That may be fine if you had a sore foot. For a more embarrassing problem, you may prefer to forget priests and try a scientific approach.

THE NEW SCIENCE

For the latest thinking, consult a doctor who follows the Hippocratic method. Hippocrates has founded a medical school on his home island of Kos. Try to find a doctor who trained there. Having learned the basics of diagnosis, he'll ask questions and examine you to try to discover what's wrong. He'll have had anatomy lessons too – probably on live subjects – so he has some idea of what's going on under your skin.

Wow!!

An anatomy lesson

Don't think the new doctors will knock Asclepius, though. Praying still has its place. They're simply more practical, following the radical line that illness isn't a punishment from the gods, but has natural causes. More shocking to local patients is the theory that doctors can cure them without divine help.

Blood letting – if you let them.

THE CURE

Your prescription will include herbal medicine and lots of rest. Like Hippocrates, many doctors believe that most ailments clear up on their own. But, like the priests, they also call for sacrifices – in the form of a healthy diet and more exercise. The doctor may be after your blood too. Literally. Even in these enlightened times, blood is believed to carry disease. If the doctor offers to open a vein, make your excuses and leave.

TOP TIPS FOR TOURISTS

No. 7: Under the knife

If you think you'll need an operation, head home. Though surgery is performed, it's all done without the aid of drugs, either to kill germs or – more significantly – your pain. Even for the Ancient Greeks, operations are a last resort. Those patients who don't die of shock on the table, usually die of infection soon after. If that doesn't put you off, just look at the instruments on the right.

HEALTH INSURANCE

Don't worry, you won't need it. If you bring enough spices to barter with, you can be sure of the doctor of your choice. Even if you don't have a bean (or, more usefully, a peppercorn), you'll still be able to get medical treatment. Under the Greek equivalent of a modern public health system, the state funds doctors so the poor can be treated free of charge.

❝ *...it arises from natural causes; men think it divine because they do not understand it.* ❞

Herodotus, a historian
(He was talking about epilepsy, known as the "Sacred Disease".)

Surgical instruments

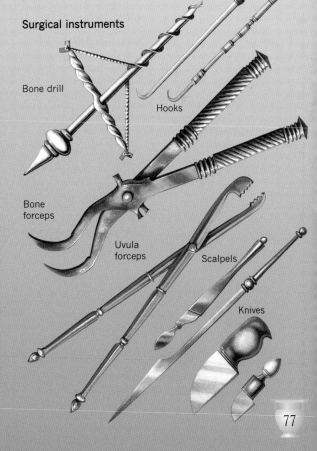

Bone drill

Hooks

Bone forceps

Uvula forceps

Scalpels

Knives

TALK THE TALK

Ancient Greece is a nation of talkers and discussion is almost the national pastime. The prime example of this is the *symposium*: far-reaching debates, on any topic you can think of, which follows dessert at a dinner party.

Male guests often bring along female companions, called *hetairai*, to amuse them. No invitation is needed, but they must be bright, pretty, young and witty. Female time tourists should grab the chance for a girls' night in.

Painting of a hetaira

TOP TIPS FOR TOURISTS

No. 8: 🗝 Riddle-me-ree

One of the most popular after-dinner games is asking riddles, with forfeits (such as drinking a glass of salty wine), if you get the answer wrong. A couple are given below, to let you know what you're in for. (The answers are upside down at the bottom of page 79.)

(1) *Don't speak and you'll express my name; say my name and you won't express me at all!*

(2) *Look at me and I'll look back, but I won't see you: I have no eyes. If you talk, my lips will move, but without a sound: I have no voice.*

KOTTABOS 🗝

For modern males, the *symposium* might not sound like that much fun anyway. But don't worry – it isn't all talk. You'll be entertained with music, dancing, acrobatics and the much-loved game, *kottabos*.

If you play a sport which involves throwing objects at a target, you'll have a head start. The steps to the game are shown below. Try to get it right first time, because the worse you are, the more you'll drink.

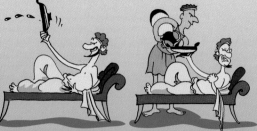

1. Don't finish your drink to the very last mouthful.

2. Instead, swirl the dregs around the bowl.

3. Hurl the contents at a target.

4. Miss and get your bowl refilled.

Tokens with a solid middle mean "innocent".

A PHILOSOPHY MATCH

Philosophy comes from the Greek word for "lover of knowledge". The earliest philosophers studied everything. But, in recent times, the study has been refined to consider the purpose of the universe and the meaning of life. If you want to hear the moral and philosophical questions of the day being discussed, head for any marketplace. Philosophers gather crowds of students around them – too big a gathering for any house – so they meet in the open air.

Tokens with a hollow middle mean "guilty".

GUILTY!

Female tourists, fed up at being left out of the *symposium*, could watch a trial. Remember, though, only citizens vote on the verdict. With no lawyers, citizens conduct their own cases. Some even hire writers (don't worry, all speeches are timed). The outcome is decided by an odd number of men, to prevent a 50:50 split, and there are several hundred on the jury. (A dozen would be too easy to bribe.)

A SPOTTER'S GUIDE TO PHILOSOPHERS

Socrates

Socrates: the father of philosophy, you may only know of Socrates as a bald old man with a long beard. At the time of your visit, he's about 35. Grab the chance to see him in action before his fame spreads. Just look for the ugly philosopher discussing truth, good and evil.

Plato

Plato: a pupil of Socrates, who will write down his teacher's ideas and develop his own on the ideal way to run a state.

Aristotle

Aristotle: a pupil of Plato (born after your visit) with a broad knowledge of politics and science.

Stoics: named after the *stoa* (porch) where they meet. Pass by and you'll hear them extol the benefits of living a calm life.

Diogenes

Diogenes: founder of the group known as *Cynics*, who don't believe in rules and dislike too much wealth. At least Diogenes lives his beliefs. He's recently moved into a large jar.

TEMPLES

On a trip here, you don't just visit the houses of famous people: you can tour the homes of gods. The Greeks believe the gods are just like humans, only more so. They even share the same needs, including having somewhere to live. Other churches may be places to worship. Greek temples are the godly version of luxury apartments (though without the kitchen or bathroom). In fact, most people pray at home, mainly heading to the temples to celebrate festivals and holidays.

BIGGER AND BETTER

Early temples weren't that luxurious as homes go. At first, a god was lucky if he got more than one room. As time went on, designers became more ambitious.

The first temples were simply a cella (room) with a porch and pillar entrance. The cella housed the god's statue, but not much else.

Later, more elaborate temples were built, with – wait for it – a porch at the back as well as the front.

Finally, designers introduced the peristyle (reasoning that if eight pillars were good, 34 must be better).

RITES & WRONGS

While visiting a temple, you may want to enter into the spirit of the thing and pray to a god.* Take a present. It needn't be flashy, but find out which gifts your god likes. (Most gods are notoriously fussy.)

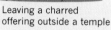

Leaving a charred offering outside a temple

Luckily, priests are usually on hand to advise you and you'll find them very approachable. Around here, they're like teachers or doctors: being a priest is just a job. At work, they may be holy; at home, they're like everyone else.

TOP TIPS FOR TOURISTS

No. 9: Let us pray

Calling upon a god isn't simply a case of kneeling down, with hands together. You address most gods with your arms high above your head, hands to the sky. (Unless you're trying to catch the attention of an Underworld god, when your palms should face the ground.) If you're addressing a sky god, face East; for a marine god, face the sea. It's largely a matter of common sense. (And if your prayers are ignored, try turning around.)

* There are plenty to choose: see pages 112-113.

THE PARTHENON

With the Classical Period, temple design is in its heyday. And the best example is the **Parthenon**, built between 447 and 438BC. If you see only one temple, make it this one. Dedicated to *Athene Parthenos*, patron goddess of Athens, the Parthenon sits high above the city. Of all the temples on the Acropolis, this is the star attraction and well worth the climb.

> ❝ *Zeus, give us what is good for us, whether we have asked for it or not, and keep us far from evil, even if we should ask for it.* ❞

A prayer by Socrates

In her right hand Athene holds a statuette of Nike, goddess of victory. Her left rests on a shield supported by a serpent.

Before you stagger in, catch your breath by looking at the incredible marble sculptures decorating the outside of the temple. They're the work of Pheidias, one of the great artists of the day. Come shortly after 438BC and they'll still be new enough for you to see the paint dry. Inside, one sight stands head and shoulders above the rest – and you: the statue of *Athene Parthenos*.

The statue of Athene, inside the Parthenon

The statue is said to have cost more than the entire temple – up close, you can see why.

Though the figure is made of wood and ivory, her dress is made of beaten gold.

The statue stands 12m (40ft) high. You might want to take binoculars to see her face (just don't get spotted).

FESTIVALS

Whatever time of year you visit, your trip is bound to coincide with a festival. With no weekends off, festivals are the only breaks the Greeks get. Basically parties for the gods enjoyed by humans, festivals offer music, drama, sports and plenty of food. (It's easy to forget their main goal is persuading gods to grant prayers.)

The Panathenaic procession

BEST OF THE FESTS

If you're in Athens over the summer, look out for the *Panathenaea*, held each year for Athene. Every four years it becomes the Great Panathenaea and lasts for six days. It's a great chance to dress up: even Athene gets a new frock. Music and dancing are followed by sports, with olive oil as prizes. Highlight of the festival is a procession to the Acropolis.

TWO GODS AND A TREE

Most festivals finish up at the temples on the **Acropolis**. At the site of what will be the Erectheion, you'll be standing on the spot of a legendary contest. For it's here, so the story goes, that Poseidon and Athene fought over who should be the city's patron.

Poseidon promised the city vast wealth through sea trade and conjured up a spring of sea water. Athene offered prosperity from farming and simply planted an olive tree. Athene was declared the winner and Athens was born. You can still see her tree growing in the courtyard, one of the city's most sacred spots.

A new dress of gold is carried by boat to Athene's statue on the Acropolis.

Dancers, musicians, soldiers and priests all process along the Panathenaic Way.

Important citizens lead the parade, followed by the offering bearers.

The Panathenaic procession leaves from the Dipylon Gate: just follow the crowds.

One hundred cows are led to the Acropolis where they're sacrificed.

THE PICK OF THE REST

Come in February and you'll be here for the *Anthesteria*. Wine from the previous year's harvest is sold and a statue of Dionysus is carried through the streets to his temple. On the last day, banquets are prepared for the spirits of the dead and placed on household altars.

In a festival similar to "Trick or Treating", children go from door to door for fruit and cakes. (But there are no tricks and the closest they get to dressing up is carrying poles wound with wool.) If you fancy a night-time festival, celebrate *Hephaestia*. Held for *Hephaestus* (blacksmith of the gods), in November, teams of runners compete by torchlight.

TOP TIPS FOR TOURISTS

No. 10: Hungry for hamburgers?

Like all good festivals, fast food is available. If your money's running out and you crave meat, try to be near the head of any procession as it arrives at a temple for the sacrifice. Once the cattle have been slaughtered, they're cooked and the meat handed out to festival-goers. (Of course, you'll need to bring your own ketchup and buns.)

" *When I was seven I carried the sacred symbols... when I was grown up handsome I carried the sacred basket...* **"**

Chorus of women from the play "Lysistrata" by Aristophanes

FESTIVAL CALENDAR

Month		Festival	God/goddess*
Hekatombaeon	July-August	Panathenaea	Athene
Metageitnion	August-September	Metageitnia	Apollo
Boedromion	September-October	Boedromia	Apollo
Pyanepsion	October-November	Pyanepsia	Apollo
Maimakterion	November-December	Maimakteria	Zeus
Poseideon	December-January	Poseidonia	Poseidon
Gamelion	January-February	Gamelia	Zeus & Hera
Anthesterion	February-March	Anthesteria	Dionysus
Elaphobelion	March-April	Elaphobelia	Artemis
Thargelion	May-June	Thargelia	Artemis & Apollo
Skirophorion	June-July	Skirophoria	Demeter & Persephone

* For more on the gods, see pages 112-113.

THE PLAY'S THE THING

The most serious Greek plays are tragedies. With their grand themes (murder, conflict, blood all over the dinner table), they could easily turn into gore-fests. Don't worry if you're squeamish. Violence takes place in the wings with a narrator telling you what's happening. The odd "dead" body may be carted on stage, but that's as gruesome as it gets.

An actor "corpsing"

LIGHT RELIEF

If doom and gloom are not for you, try comedies, or "satyr" plays. Comedies, as the name implies, are the opposite of tragedies and focus on lighter concerns. Much of the fun, however, is at the expense of the stars and politics of the day (not unlike pantomimes). To get every joke, you'll probably have to bone up on current affairs first. "Satyr" plays are comedies which poke fun at tragedies. The name comes from some of the cast who dress as satyrs: half-men, half-beasts.

A buffoon in a comedy

A satyr acting in a tragi-comedy or a comi-tragedy.

ATHENS DRAMA FESTIVAL

Drama addicts should visit Athens during the *Dionysia*. Named after Dionysus (the god of wine), it's a combined religious and drama fest and lasts for five days. After the first day's processions and sacrifices come the drama competitions. Each year, three tragedy and five comedy playwrights make the shortlist. You may see the première of a play which will still be being performed in 2,500 years' time.

BIRTH OF THE PLAY

The Dionysia began as an ancient countryside festival. A group of singers and dancers, called the "chorus" and all wearing masks, enacted various legends. There could be up to 50 of them, reciting in unison. Every so often, one actor would have a solo. Gradually, the chorus grew smaller and three actors became full-time soloists, sharing up to 45 parts. Now, the dialogue between soloists is the most important part. The chorus stays in the background, passing the odd comment and linking events.

A tragic actor

THE "MODERN" STAGE

At first, plays were put on in the marketplace. The audience sat in wooden stands put up for the festival each year. But one year the stands collapsed, killing several of the audience, so a permanent, open-air arena was built of stone. Drama is now so popular, similar arenas can be found in every major city in the Greek world.

An open-air arena

The actors change in here.

Altar

Male and female parts are played by men.

Chorus members sing and dance in the orchestra (dancing floor).

The arenas can hold up to 18,000 spectators.

SETTING THE SCENE

In such vast arenas, from a distance the actors look little more than performing fleas. So, the costumes are designed to let you know who they're playing. Happy characters are dressed brightly. Tragic ones wear dark clothes. The costumes are often heavily padded and actors wear platform boots and huge wigs to help them stand out.

Actors wear painted masks made of stiffened fabric or cork, so you can see their expressions from a distance. The large mouths amplify the actors' voices.

TOP TIPS FOR TOURISTS

No. 11: Box office

Instead of tickets, you'll need tokens. These have a letter showing which row your seat is in. Blocks of seats are divided into city districts, so if you want to sit with friends from another part of town, buy your tickets together. They cost two *obols** each. You should also check when you book if females in your party may sit with you. And don't worry if you're stuck at the back. The arenas have fantastic acoustics. Wherever you sit, you'll hear every word.

*One *obol* = 1/6 *drachma*; tickets cost about a third of an average day's pay

ENTERTAINMENT

Greek drama isn't to everyone's taste, but there are plenty of other pastimes and diversions, from the high-brow music, poetry and dance to the low-brow board games and games of chance.

The youngest tourists aren't left out either. Toddling siblings can be amused with numerous wooden toys, including dolls, hoops, rattles and tops. And if you're a whizz with yoyos back home, here's your chance to shine. Children here have yoyos too, though not flashing plastic ones.

Shakers

Hand-held drum called a timpanon

Cymbals

Panpipes

A horn

The lyre, a hand-held harp

Pipes called auloi

Getting into the party spirit

MUSIC & MOVEMENT

You're in for a surprise where Greek music is concerned: no one in modern times has ever heard any. Because there's no written music from the period, it's impossible to recreate in the 21st century. The instruments should be largely familiar, even if the sound they make together isn't. The harp, cymbals and panpipes are all around in a similar form today.

But look out for the *auloi*; not so much an instrument as a party trick. It's made up of two pipes played by one man at the same time.

You may be tempted to dance to the music, but don't try any modern routines. People here consider dancing one of the highest art forms and expect it to be always both beautiful and expressive.

RAPPING RHAPSODES

For the tone-deaf there is always literature, though even here, poetry has a musical slant. It truly is performance art, usually read aloud but often sung or chanted with a musical backing. Think of it as the forerunner of rapping. In fact the men who earn their living by reciting poetry at religious festivals are called *rhapsodes*.

Painting of a rhapsode

If you'd like to pick up extra cash by busking this way, you'll need a good memory. *Rhapsodes* know the epic poems (one of which fills several books) by heart. If they ask for requests, suggest *The Iliad* or *The Odyssey*. These two epics of Greek history were written 400 years ago by the poet Homer.

GAMES

If the above is too cultural for you, there are less intellectual pursuits. One very popular game is "Blind Man's Buff" (think "Tag" with a blindfold), enjoyed by adults and children alike. For the energetic, there's a ball game similar to hockey. But if you prefer your fun sitting down, try dice or knuckle bones.

JUST THE ONE...

One activity everyone enjoys is a drink or two of (watered-down) wine. Before you're tempted to follow suit, you might like to read the words of warning in the quote below. It's a saying currently doing the rounds in Athens.

> **"** *The first cup means health, the second pleasure. The third cup is for sleep... then wise men go home. The fourth cup means rudeness, the fifth shouting. The sixth is disorder... The seventh... black eyes and the eighth brings a police summons.* **"**

For one drinker, the party is definitely over...

TOP TIPS FOR TOURISTS

No. 12: Amuse a Muse

Crucial to any artist, whether writer, dancer or musician, is inspiration. The Ancient Greeks believe this comes from nine goddesses called Muses, each responsible for a separate art form. If your verses don't scan, your pipe sounds like a hoarse duck, or you dance with two left feet, try calling on one of them for help.

ART & SCULPTURE

Even if you have little interest in museums, you can't avoid Greek art. Sculptures are everywhere: in homes and temples, even the street. Early statues copied the Egyptian style and were admittedly stiff stuff. But in recent years art has undergone a makeover, and some of the work being produced is amazing.

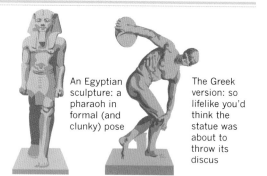

An Egyptian sculpture: a pharaoh in formal (and clunky) pose

The Greek version: so lifelike you'd think the statue was about to throw its discus

THE NEW PERFECTIONISM

Classical sculptors are perfecting the knack of showing the human body, caught in a moment in time. Statues are noted for their beauty and serenity; even those in athletic poses have a flowing grace. As for the clothes draped around the bodies: you may have to touch them to prove they're made of stone not fabric.

This famous boxer was actually made later than your trip. But it's a good example of the more realistic direction sculptures will take.

TOP TIPS FOR TOURISTS

No. 13: What a relief

A life-sized marble statue may be impractical to cart home. But if you're hooked on Greek art, don't worry. Mini versions of temple carvings are made as offerings. You could commission one for your wall. Small terracotta figures in scenes from daily life are also popular – and would easily fit in a backpack.

SELF-EXPRESSION

Greek artists are especially adept at portraying human emotions and eager to show off by sculpting stars of the day. They do a fine line in beautiful goddesses, too. Pheidias is the name on everyone's lips. Apart from his statue of Athene on the Acropolis, he made the incredible one of Zeus at Olympia (see page 98).

PRODUCTION LINE

Statues are carved from marble or limestone, or shaped from bronze. The stone ones are cut roughly into shape as they're quarried, to make them easier to transport to the workshops. If you're quiet, a sculptor may let you watch him at work.

Once carved, marble statues are painted to create a lifelike appearance. Glass or stones are used for eyes and statues are even accessorized, with crowns, weapons and jewels, all made from bronze.

Seeing a flowing figure appear from a lump of stone (if you can wait around for two months) is almost a supernatural experience.

A sculptor's workshop

FACTORY FINISH

Athenian sculptors have a growing reputation. As their fame spreads, demand for the statues has been outstripping supply. Factories are now springing up at quarries, so sculptures can be produced on-site and exported all over the Mediterranean.

Carving out a scene of gods to be built into a temple

A RELIEF FROM STATUES

Statues aren't the only expression of Greek art. Sculptors also carve slabs of stone with "reliefs": scenes with figures which stand out against a flat background. They're mostly found on temples (check out the Parthenon for some fantastic examples). To take a more unusual art tour, visit the local graveyard. Athens, especially, is known for its spectacular gravestones.

ARCHITECTURE & BUILDINGS

Greek architecture will make an impression on everyone over the years, from the Romans (who'll copy everything they can get their hands on), to Renaissance Italians, modern designers and architects.

The architecture is all based on mathematics. The proportions of Ancient Greek buildings, the height and width of columns, for example, are carefully calculated. It's this that gives the buildings their air of well-balanced elegance. In layman's terms: they look good.

BACK TO BASICS

All public buildings (private homes aren't so important) follow the same basic design. A series of vertical columns is topped with a horizontal beam (the lintel). This is said to be a development from much earlier buildings, where tree trunks were used to support the roofs.

The Doric style is a simple design, with broad, plain columns.

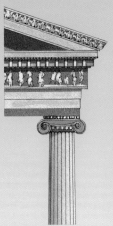

The Ionic is more elegant and decorative than the Doric. Columns are slender and their tops ("capitals" to use the technical term), are decorated.

There are some variations, though. The different styles are called "orders" and there are two main ones to look out for: *Doric* and *Ionic*. As you sightsee, see how many of each you can spot. You get extra points if you find *Corinthian* or *Aeolic* columns (both forms of the Ionic). They're not used all that often.

TOP TIPS FOR TOURISTS

No. 14: Casing the joint?

Be careful not to hang around the back of a temple. It's where the treasury is located. The guards may not believe your excuse that you're just an architecture fan – and Athenian jails are not places you'd want to visit.

Corinthian column

Aeolic column

BUILDING WORKS

All cities are usually undergoing some major construction and the Greek city-states are no exception. The only things missing from the ancient skyline are cranes. Public buildings are continually being commissioned and a Greek building site is an eye-opening experience.

Most buildings are constructed from marble or limestone, with wooden beams supporting the roof. Roofs have terracotta or, more rarely, marble tiles and the outsides of buildings are decorated with painted statues and sculpted reliefs.

Since Pericles is having all of the temples on the Acropolis rebuilt, you'll have the chance to see at least one being put up. Stop for a while and watch the builders at work. They do an impressive job of putting up these vast structures with neither cranes nor cement.

A temple building site

Blocks are joined together with metal rods called dowels, which fit through the middle of each block.

Stones are carved with mallet and chisel and hoisted into place using ropes and pulleys.

BATTLE OF THE BULGE

When you're standing by a temple, its columns towering over you, take a closer look. Seen from below, a column with completely straight sides appears thinner in the middle. To combat this, architects have designed a bulge into their columns. They then go in at the top, drawing your eye up to the magnificent carvings around the roof.

Columns with and without a bulge

91

ARCADES & THE AGORA

Shopping: love it or hate it, in Ancient Greece you can't avoid it. The *agora*, or marketplace, is at the heart of every Greek city. It's not a bad place to start your sightseeing in each new town. You can stock up on any supplies that are running low at the same time. It's also the place to change your coins into the local currency.

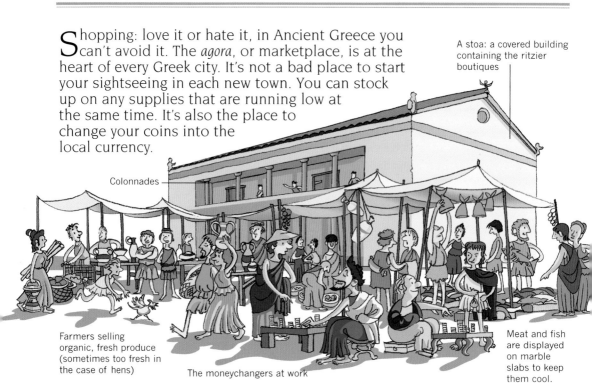

A stoa: a covered building containing the ritzier boutiques

Colonnades

Farmers selling organic, fresh produce (sometimes too fresh in the case of hens)

The moneychangers at work

Meat and fish are displayed on marble slabs to keep them cool.

CHANGING MONEY

Before you can shop, you'll need a moneychanger. Look for the wealthy men behind tables (and piles of money). If your Greek is up to it, you could just ask for the *trapezitai* (which means "table men"). They'll change coins from all of the city-states, although – like *bureaux de change* everywhere – they charge commission. And check your coins closely. Worn coins which are too light are rejected by traders.

It's worth noting that the *trapezitai* also act as bankers. Deposit some change with them and you won't have to lug heavy purse-loads of coins around with you.

SHOPPING ARCADES

If you prefer upmarket shopping to an open market, head for the covered buildings called *stoae*. Stores lined up behind rows of colonnades (columns), offer everything from pricey jewels to lamps. You can also pick up offerings, such as incense or honeycakes, for any temples you may plan to visit. But you can't browse; you'll have to squint. Most shops are simply open rooms with a counter where the front wall should be.

UNDER THE COLONNADES

The shady colonnades are an ideal place to meet friends. You could buy a snack in the market, but remember: only the lower classes and slaves eat in public.

THE PRODUCE POLICE

You may have been to markets whose stall holders weren't all above board. Traders in the agora are monitored by various officials. In Athens, ten *metronomoi* are also chosen each year to check the accuracy of traders' weights and measures. And if you're unhappy with the quality of an item you've bought, complain to the *agoranomoi*: the Greeks' trading standards officers.

An Athenian coin

SLAVES FOR SALE

One "product" you might prefer not to see on sale is people. But, as in many of the ancient civilizations, slavery is a fact of life. Not even Athenian citizens are immune. If they're captured as prisoners of war, they can be sold on as slaves to citizens in another city-state.

Slave auction on a podium

A successful bidder

TOP TIPS FOR TOURISTS

No. 15: Retail therapy for men

Back home, men may leave the shopping to women. They don't get away with that here. Men do almost all of it (and that includes buying food). Female tourists may be more astonished to learn that they won't be allowed to buy things over a certain amount. If an expensive souvenir takes your fancy, you will have to persuade a male companion to buy it for you.

WORKSHOPS & CRAFTSMEN

Close to the agora you'll find local craftsmen. They often set up shop (and home) nearby, to encourage customers to visit. If you want something made, such as a pair of shoes (and you'll be around to collect them), this is where to place your order. Craftsmen often cluster together, with all the potters in one area, for example. It certainly makes life easier when comparing prices and styles.

POT MANIA

Ancient Greek pots are exported all over the known world. You might think about buying some: they'll become collector's items. The first pots made after the Dark Ages were simply decorated with geometric patterns (and, later, human and animal figures). But, about 200 years ago, contact with the wider world led to a craze for Egyptian designs.

These days, pots show scenes from myths and daily life. Take a pot instead of a photo for a snapshot of Greek life to show friends at home. (Even if you brought a camera, using it might lead to awkward questions.) Early examples have black figures on a red background.

RED IS THE NEW BLACK

The latest fashion is for "red-figure ware". The clay used turns red when fired. Red-figure pots are painted black with spaces left for the figures. When the pots come out of the kiln, the painted areas have stayed black but the blank figure shapes have turned red. Finer details are then added with white or dark red paint.

Two examples of red-figure ware

POTS FOR EVERY OCCASION: A SHOPPER'S GUIDE

Aryballos Flask for perfumed oils		**Kylix** Drinking cup
Alabastron Flask for perfumed oils and ointments		**Skyphos** Drinking cup
Loutrophoros Ceremonial vase to carry water for a bridal bath		**Kantharos** Drinking cup
Pyxis Medicine or cosmetics box		**Calyx Krater*** For turning water into wine...
Amphora* Storage jar for oil or wine		**Volute Krater*** Krater with spiral handles
Hydria* Water carrier		**Oinochoe** Serving jug for wine

* If you want one of these, take a friend. They're too big for one person to carry.

SOUVENIR GUIDE

There's nothing worse when you're away (apart from the unavoidable tourist tummy), than traipsing around looking for things to take home as gifts. That huge *krater*, such a familiar sight at meal times, may well look out of place in your mother's kitchen. And trendy as your dad likes to think he is, he can hardly go to a football game in a tunic.

Your best bet is to go for light, easily portable items. (It may sound obvious but look at all the tourists struggling home through customs and you'll see it needs repeating.)

Impulse purchases are never a good idea.

Ideal choices are statuettes or small pieces of pottery. If you do go for a statuette, avoid the junk specifically designed for the tourist market.

Other gifts you could consider include high-quality embroidered robes, rings and brooches, and cosmetics. If you're really stuck, there's always olive oil. But pack it carefully or you'll end up with soggy, greasy clothes and no gift.

> 66 *You will find everything sold together in the same place at Athens.* 99

Euboulos, a poet

TOP TIPS FOR TOURISTS

No. 16: Sparing Granny's blushes

Most Greeks have a remarkably relaxed attitude to the human body. This is perhaps inevitable in a place so hot you wear as little as possible. It does mean, however, that they are quite happy to plaster all sorts of dubious images over their pottery.

Many vases have very explicit scenes (red-figure ware in particular), so choose souvenirs for your grandparents carefully. Unless you have broad-minded elderly relatives, it might be safer to bring them back olives.

CENSORED

A risqué wine cooler

PIRAEUS, PORT OF ATHENS

Just 9 kms (5½ miles) southwest of Athens lies the city's port, **Piraeus**. All of the imports and most visitors entering the city arrive here first. If you've spent a few quiet days on a beach, go to Piraeus for excitement. The place buzzes with activity. You can mingle with merchants, share a drink with a sailor or bask in the sun watching shipbuilders at work.

You'll see people from every nation, and fellow tourists from Phoenicia, Egypt, Persia and Babylon. Don't be surprised if the locals call them "barbarians", despite their often elegant and cultured appearance.

"Barbarian" is the name given to all foreigners, because, to the Greeks, they seem to say "baa-baa".

A WALL WALK

Set out for Piraeus from Athens and you'll follow one of the major sights, the **Long Walls** (*Makra Teiche*). Work began on them in 460BC to link the city to the port, thanks to Pericles. He saw the disaster waiting to happen if an enemy cut off Athens from its navy and port, the main source of supplies.

66 *From all the lands, everything enters.* 99

Thucydides (a politician and historian) describing Piraeus

A scene from the docks at Piraeus

Tasting the produce

Traders

TOP TIPS FOR TOURISTS

No. 17: Bird's eye view

For the best overview of the walls and a chance to see all the way back to Athens, climb **Munychia Hill**. Topped by a temple to Athene Munychia, it offers the best view in the area.

SNACKS & SOUVENIRS

Piraeus is where to find last-minute mementos, plus lunch to sustain what could be a mammoth shop. For really extravagant buys, such as silk, head to a warehouse on the docks. Shipments are stored here before being sent around the country. Look for items which didn't survive the sea journey that well. You may pick up a bargain. To see the range of imports and where they come from (and to write a shopping list), check the map:

BRIEF HISTORY OF PIRAEUS

Piraeus, with its three natural ports and closeness to Athens, is one of the city's biggest assets. But this wasn't realized and exploited until 493BC. Themistocles, a ruler of Athens, had a wall built around the city and turned it into a naval headquarters. Piraeus has been redesigned recently, to make better use of the three ports: Karanthos, Munychia and Zea.

The imports flooding Piraeus

ITALY: wood, grain, meat, pottery

CHINA: silk

Black Sea

PHOENICIA: ointment, dye, flour, dates

Athens

CYPRUS: grain, oil wood, copper

SICILY: grain, cheese, pigs

CRETE: cyprus wood

INDIA: gems, ebony, spices, elephants

CARTHAGE: wool, rugs, cushions

EGYPT: grain, gems, linen, ivory, papyrus

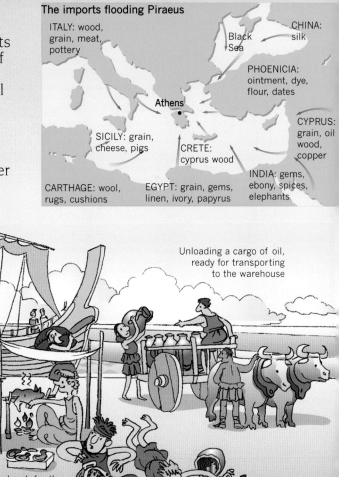

Unloading a cargo of oil, ready for transporting to the warehouse

Catch of the day: fish is plentiful and very fresh

Cooking lunch for the sailors, dockhands and tourists

THE OLYMPIC GAMES

The original Olympic Games began way back in 776BC and are part of the Pan-Hellenic games, the sports fixture of the year. Held at **Olympia** every four years, they last five days, the focus of a festival to celebrate the god Zeus. Messengers travel to every Greek state announcing the date and warring states call a three-month truce so you, and every other tourist, can travel to Olympia safely.

SPECTATOR SPORT FOR MEN

When you arrive, pitch your tent at the camp by the river, then wander around to take in the atmosphere. Masses of things are provided for the celebrities and visitors who descend during the Games. You'll find souvenir stalls lining the roads by the stadium. There are sightseeing tours, shrines to visit, even poetry recitals.

And don't forget the religious side of things. Pilgrims worship at Zeus' temple, worth visiting for the ivory and gold statue of Zeus, standing 13m (43ft) high. It's a good idea to take a gift – it need only be incense or wine. But set out early. People start lining up to get in at dawn.

The Olympic village

Training area for jumping and wrestling

The Gymnasium: a training ground for running and throwing events

Temple of Zeus

The stadium

YOUR GUIDE TO EVENTS

WARNING! These athletes are clothed. In real life, they wear nothing but a layer of oil (to protect against sunburn).

Running: the oldest event, the stadium track is 192m (640ft) long; made of clay covered with sand. There are three races: *stade* (1 length); *diaulos* (2 lengths) and *dolichos* (20 or 24 lengths).

Wrestling: fans get to see three types: **upright**, where an opponent must be thrown to the ground three times; **ground**, where one fighter must simply give in; and **pankration**, the most dangerous, a mix of wrestling and boxing. Only two tactics are banned: biting and eye-gouging.

Pentathlon: made up of five events – running, wrestling, jumping, discus and javelin throwing – the goal is to find the best all-rounder.

Boxing: you'll need almost as much stamina as the fighters, as boxing matches can last for hours. They're only decided when one fighter loses consciousness or concedes defeat – so most blows are aimed at the head and virtually any blow with the hand is OK.

Chariot & horse racing: chariot drivers race 12 laps around two posts in the ground. Jockeys ride bareback over 1.2km (¾ mile). Both can be nasty as accidents are common.

Arena for chariot and horse races

INSIDE THE STADIUM

Judges watch events from seats in a special stand in the stadium. You'll simply stand. But the stadium holds 40,000, so you should get in.

You get an excellent view of the Games from the grassy slopes surrounding the stadium.

Track events in the stadium open the first day. A trumpet blasts, the judges take their seats, then more trumpets precede the announcement of the first race. As only citizens and non-criminals can take part, an announcer then calls out the names of the competitors. After each event, the announcer gives the name of the winner, his father's name and his city.

Statue of a female Greek runner

GAMES FOR WOMEN

Only men may compete in the Games. Married women can't even watch, on pain of death. Single women aren't exactly welcome, either. Instead, they have their own festival, *Heraia*, for the goddess Hera. Also held every four years, it has running races for girls of various ages.

WINNING SPONSORSHIP

Prizes are given on the last day of the Games and include ribbons, olive wreaths and palm branches. Athletes are meant to seek only the glory of competing and winning, but many become professionals. Cities gain prestige from sponsoring successful athletes, so they put up statues of them and make them payments on the quiet.

Grateful city officials and a winning athlete

TOP TIPS FOR TOURISTS

No. 18: The judges' decision is final

Though there are many rules and regulations for competitors, as a spectator you need only remember one. Never disagree with the judges in public. Cries of, "Oh come off it, ref! Are you blind?" may be OK at home. At the Games, you risk a fine – or worse.

ORACLES & OTHER MYSTERIES

Unsure what to do next? Visit an oracle! It's a good introduction to an important part of Greek life and you may get some hints on planning the rest of your stay. Oracles are the Greek way of seeking advice from the gods. Rather confusingly, when a local refers to an oracle, he could mean one of three things: a priestess speaking for a god; the sacred place where she speaks; or the message itself. Whichever it is, oracles are consulted for all major decisions, and some minor ones.

THE ORACLE AT DELPHI

The most famous – and the one to visit – is the oracle at **Delphi**. It's about 160km (100 miles) from Athens, built around a sacred spring on the slopes of Mount Parnassus. Here, the god Apollo gives his answers via a priestess called the *Pythia*. Originally, she only gave sittings once a year. But the oracle is now so in demand, hearings take place once a month and two extra "Pythians" have been taken on.

You can ask anything you like and questions range from, "Has my jug been stolen?" to "Should I expand my business?" First, however, Apollo must like you. You'll be asked to make a sacrifice to decide this (and you'll have to pay). Assuming you pass the test, you'll join a line of answer-seekers, drawing lots to see who goes first.

> 66 *Unhappy people, why stay you here? Leave your homes... and flee to the ends of the earth.* 99

Herodotus, *a historian, reporting the Pythia's advice to Athenians in 480BC, just before a Persian attack*

GO-BETWEENS

You can't deal directly with the Pythia. Instead, temple priests will pass on your question and relay the answer. Before you give them the question, make sure you've had a quick dip in the **Castalian Spring**. Like all priests, the Delphic ones are sticklers for cleanliness. You won't be able to see what goes on after you've asked your question, but the picture below should give you some idea.

Inside the inner sanctum

The Pythia sits on a tripod and inhales the smoke of burning laurel leaves.

Then she goes into a trance and gives Apollo's answer. Even the priests don't get to watch – she's hidden behind a curtain.

SOOTHSAYERS

If you're turned down by Apollo, all is not lost. The Greeks don't only look to the gods for answers. Just ask to be directed to the nearest seer or soothsayer: they can see into the future. Not convinced? There are plenty of stories to prove their accuracy, including the legend of Cassandra, a princess of Troy.* She foretold an attack on the city. The Trojans didn't believe a word – until the attack began.

Cassandra was proved right when the Trojans were attacked by Greek soldiers who'd hidden in a giant wooden horse.

THE OMEN

The reliance on the supernatural doesn't stop there. Another option is to consult a "diviner" (reader of signs), who is usually a priest.

1. Reading tokens with symbolic signs

2. Reading signs in nature, such as the flight of birds

3. The gory task of reading the innards of a sacrificed animal

Of course, you'll have to pay for the privilege of their advice. Since the omens can only answer "yes" or "no" you may decide to keep your coin and toss it for an answer. Heads they win, tails you lose...

MYSTERY CULTS

Some citizens join a cult to find the meaning of life. Sadly, the one thing cults have in common is that members are sworn to secrecy. Tourists are definitely <u>not</u> welcome. The closest you'll get is to watch a procession. Each *Boedromion* (September-October), members and wannabes of the Eleusinian cult walk from Athens to Eleusis during their initiation ceremony.

TOP TIPS FOR TOURISTS
No. 19: Pythian puzzle

Advice from the Pythia is only the start. She's tricky. Answers are so cleverly phrased, you'd think Apollo was trying to cover all bases. Be warned by the tale of Croesus, a king who asked if he should invade Persia (present-day Iran).

Told he would "destroy a great empire", Croesus attacked and suffered a terrible defeat. When he complained, he was told he had destroyed a great empire: his. (Don't be put off. Plenty of seers hang around the temple to interpret the Pythia's words.)

* An ancient city described in *The Iliad*, a poem by the Greek poet Homer.

HOT METAL

If oracles prove just too spiritual, here's the perfect antidote: a trip to the mines at **Laurion**. Sited 65km (40 miles) south of Athens, this is materialism at its best (or worst). Much of the city's wealth comes from the mine with its rich seam of silver-lead. (For those who collect statistics, Laurion is the largest individual supplier of silver to the ancient world.)

The mines are owned by the Athenian state, but leased to private contractors keen to make the quickest buck for the cheapest outlay. Conditions are harsh. Slave-miners work ten-hour shifts and usually die after only three or four years of doing the job.

A view of the mine underground (You won't be allowed down.)

The mine is reached via an extremely narrow shaft.

Metal is hauled to the surface in baskets.

Ventilation shaft

Oil lamp

Access is so restricted in some places that miners have to work on their backs.

Up to 20,000 miners work in the mines at any one time.

ABOVE GROUND

You won't be able to see any underground activity, but plenty takes place on the surface. The silver-lead ore leaves the mine with a lot of mine still on it. So, the next stage is washing off the debris, something you may well be able to watch.

Slaves pound the ore with clubs, to break it up from the rock. This is a dusty business and it's a good idea to bring a light scarf to cover your face if you want to watch.

Finally, the crumbly mix is flooded with water and sifted, to rinse the rock dust from the ore.

Breaking up the rock and silver-lead ore

BRONZED OFF

Silver (and gold) are only used for money and precious items. Most everyday Greek objects, and many statues, are made of bronze, a mix of tin and copper. Metalsmiths usually work from home, though in Athens they have their own quarter.

If you want to watch a smith at work, he probably won't mind – but you might like instead to glance at their various ways of working (shown below). Parts of the job are tricky, and ill-timed questions won't be appreciated.

1. Hammering method: sheets of bronze are hammered into shape, then riveted together around a wooden core.

2. Casting method: melted bronze is poured into a cast and left to harden.

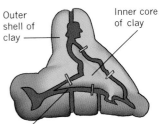

Outer shell of clay

Inner core of clay

Wax model of a boy on a dolphin between the two layers of clay

3. Lost wax method: a wax statue is shaped around a clay core, covered in more clay and heated. The wax melts and is replaced with melted bronze. Once this has set, the outer clay shell is removed.

TOP TIPS FOR TOURISTS

No. 20: Slaves for life

Some slaves in Athens (usually craftsmen), are paid for their work. So, if you're happy with the goods or service provided, you can tip them knowing the money will help buy their freedom. This doesn't happen in Laurion. The mine owners don't want the slaves to have even a chance of leaving. Slip a slave some money and his overseer will pocket it – and probably punish you both.

THE IRON MEN

Iron has only been in use for about 500 years, but it's the preferred metal for weapons and tools, because it's so tough. Iron hasn't replaced bronze entirely though, as it's much more expensive to produce.

Smiths have to heat the iron ore at a very high temperature to extract the metal, which then needs its impurities beaten out.

A furnace for smelting iron

SPARTA: KEEP OUT!

It may seem odd (if not pointless), to read in a guide book about a city which you cannot visit. But if you're wise, reading about Sparta (in some other, safer, city-state), is the closest you'll get.

The Spartans' reputation is such that their name is known in the 21st century: "a spartan room". However bleak the phrase seems, believe us: the real thing is worse. Just reading these pages should convince you that (a) the Spartans are not people to mess with and (b) Sparta is the last place to visit as part of a relaxing vacation.

HARD AS NAILS

The city of Sparta is the strongest military power in Greece. Even though not currently at war, it stays on permanent alert. Every man must join the army, facing a lifetime of training and fighting. But living conditions are basic and uncomfortable for all. Spartans eat plain food and wear the cheapest clothes so there's no risk of their being softened up.

Bronze statue of a Spartan warrior, made in the fifth century BC

TOUGH LOVE

Spartan boys start training for war young.

Boys fight to protect their reputations – and their tunics. (They only get one tunic a year.)

Boys are put in groups and elect a leader to organize them.

A Spartan's hard life begins at birth. In fact, anyone too much of a weakling doesn't get a life. Babies are carefully examined to check their strength. Any not up to scratch are left out to die of exposure. At seven, boys are sent to school where they live in barracks. For the next thirteen years, they're given weapon training, endless athletic fitness sessions and frequent beatings to check their toughness.

WOMEN'S RIGHTS

Spartan women are equally important to the war effort. It's every woman's duty to keep fit to have healthy babies. Unlike the rest of Greece, women here play many sports. They also bring up the children, seeing their husbands (who must live in the army barracks), on rare weekend leave.

FRIENDLY FIRE

Despite their military might, Sparta couldn't withstand a major war alone. So, the Spartans have made various alliances with nearby states in southern Greece. They're known collectively as the Peloponnesian League. These allies have remained independent, but will rush to Sparta's side as and when required.

HELOT OF HARDSHIP

A Spartan soldier, on a rare visit home, overseeing a slave (helot) on his farm

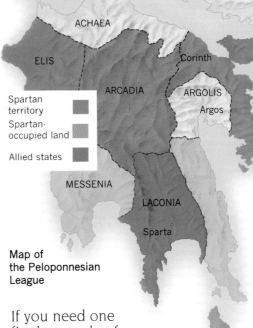

Spartan territory

Spartan-occupied land

Allied states

ACHAEA

ELIS

Corinth

ARCADIA

ARGOLIS

Argos

MESSENIA

LACONIA

Sparta

Map of the Peloponnesian League

If you need one final example of Spartan single-mindedness, consider the *helots*. These descendants of Sparta's original inhabitants are ruthlessly oppressed by their new Spartan rulers. Each Spartan soldier is given land and the helots to work it. This provides him with an income, while leaving him free to pursue his army career.

NOT ONE OF US

Only men born in Sparta are citizens. Other men are *perioikoi*: free men who nevertheless have to live in separate villages. It's the perioikoi who deal with trade and outsiders, leaving the Spartans free to fight. Even if you went to Sparta, you'd be unlikely to have much contact with the Spartans, since they keep themselves to themselves.

They're pretty much cut off from contact with the outside world too. They don't even have a system of coins, unlike other city-states. Instead, they usually barter, or trade, goods.

TOP TIPS FOR TOURISTS

No. 21: If you achieve the impossible...

...and do get into Sparta, be warned that on your return to Athens, you won't be greeted with open arms – more likely a spear point. There's currently a state of cold war between the two sides, with Athenians very nervous of Sparta's plans. They are right to be. Things will heat up when war breaks out again in 431.

GOVERNMENT & POLITICS

CRADLE OF DEMOCRACY?

Greece is often called the birthplace of democracy, but you may not recognize the original baby. Brought in by Cleisthenes, leader of Athens, in 506BC, it comes from the Greek words for "people" (*demos*) and "rule" (*kratos*). But the only people who can vote are citizens: free men with Athenian parents. Women, slaves and foreign residents are all excluded from the polls.

LOCAL GOVERNMENT

Cleisthenes also split Athens and the surrounding areas (collectively known as Attica) into groups to make it easier to govern them:

ATTICA

was divided into hundreds of small communities called *demes*.

These *demes* were organized into 30 large groups called *trittyes*. There were...

10 groups on the coast...   10 in the city (Athens)...   and 10 in the country.

The 30 *trittyes* were then split into 10 tribes called *phylai*. Each tribe (*phyle*) was made up of 3 *trittyes*: 1 from the coast, 1 from the city and 1 from the country.

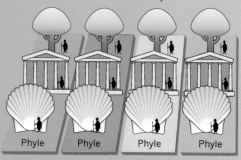

Phyle   Phyle   Phyle   Phyle

THE COUNCIL & ASSEMBLY

New laws and policies are drawn up by the Council of 500 citizens (made up of 50 men from each of the 10 *phylai* or tribes). Councillors are elected annually and each tribe takes a turn running the state day-to-day. Any proposed laws are debated by the Assembly, where every citizen has a right to speak and vote.

The Town Council

The Council meets in a round building called the Tholos.

The building is manned 24 hours a day in case of emergencies.

If you want to see Greek democracy in action, go along to the hill called the **Pnyx**. The Assembly meets here about every ten days. Not only are all citizens entitled to take part, 6,000 of them are needed for a meeting to take place at all. If too few people turn up, police are sent out to round up more voters. (Don't you get carried away and try to vote though. You'll be thrown out.)

SOLDIER POLITICIANS

The most important men in the government are *strategoi*. Basically military generals, ten are elected annually, one from each tribe. They have the job of implementing policies approved by the Assembly. But they're not all-powerful: they must answer to the Assembly for their actions and any money spent.

ANACHRONISTIC ARCHONS

You may also come across the nine *archons*, also elected every year. They used to have immense power, but, these days, they mainly take part in ceremonies. Three of them, however, still have special responsibilities:

The Polemarch Archon

In charge of offerings and special athletic contests held for men killed in war, he also deals with the legal affairs of foreign residents (known as *metics*).

The Basileus Archon

He presides over law courts; arranges religious sacrifices and renting out temple land; and organizes festivals and feasts.

The Eponymous Archon

He finds money men to finance the music and drama festivals and takes charge of inheritance lawsuits, plus the affairs of heiresses, orphans and widows.

OSTRACISM

The Athenians don't simply throw rotten eggs at politicians they're not pleased with. They banish them. Citizens meet in the Assembly once a year to vote politicians out. Everyone writes the name of the person they want kicked out on a broken piece of pot called an *ostrakon*. If a politician has more than 600 votes cast against him, he must leave Athens for 10 years.

POLITICAL GAFFE

Once, a citizen came up from the country to take part in the ostracism vote, but he couldn't write. So, he asked the stranger standing next to him to write down the name of the man he wanted banished. Unfortunately, the man he asked was the man he wanted banished...

FOREIGN POLICY

Ever since the Greeks defeated the Persians in 479BC, they've been waiting for the revenge attack. In preparation for this, various Greek states led by Athens have grouped together to form a league. The first meeting was on the island of Delos in 478BC, so they called themselves the Delian League. Members have agreed to provide ships and money for a navy, and to defend each other's territories in times of war.

THE ARMY

FROM HORSES TO HOPLITES

Originally, the most important part of the Greek army was the cavalry. And, as soldiers had to provide their own horses and weapons, it was made up of wealthy men. Foot soldiers were drawn from the poorer ranks, so their weapons were pretty makeshift. But recent years have seen the rise of *hoplites*, an elite class of foot soldiers who are much better trained and equipped.

EQUIPPED FOR BATTLE

Early hoplites wore a solid bronze body protector, but – as you need to be flexible to win a fight – modern versions combine bronze with leather. Leg guards are also made of bronze and the whole ensemble is protected from neck to thigh by a bronze and leather shield. A hoplite's main weapon is a long spear backed up by a short iron sword. It's all very expensive and paid for by hoplites themselves.

A 3m (10ft) spear of solid bronze

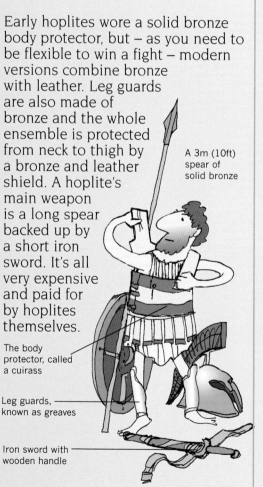

The body protector, called a cuirass

Leg guards, known as greaves

Iron sword with wooden handle

KEEP IT UNDER YOUR HAT

The helmet of the moment is the *Thracian*, made of bronze and horsehair, with long cheek pieces. Helmets have always been bronze, and usually adorned with horsehair crests, but there have been changes along the way. You might spot a couple of the older designs (shown below) in a march or parade. They're worn by die-hards who refuse to give in to current trends.

Helmets past and present

| Later Corinthian helmet | Chalcidian helmet | Thracian helmet |

AUXILIARIES

Men who can't afford the rigout of a hoplite act as back-up. They form lightly armed auxiliary units, made up of archers, stone slingers and *psiloi*, who fight with stones, clubs or whatever else is at hand.

CALL UP

Every state has its own way of raising an army. In Athens, there's the "List": men go on it at 20 and are called to active duty if there's a war. Men between 50 and 60 go onto a reserve list, to be called on in an emergency. Each of the ten tribes provides a commander, known as a *taxiarch*, and a *strategos* (general), who is elected by the Assembly. Each tribe also provides enough soldiers for one regiment.

BATTLE PLANS

Soldiers in early armies fought one-on-one. Hoplites fight in formation which needs training, discipline and above all timing. To keep them in step, a piper plays them into battle. Soldiers form a block, or *phalanx*, eight rows deep.

In battle, opposing phalanxes charge together, pushing against each other until one gives way. If a man at the front is injured or killed, the soldier behind takes his place. Each soldier is covered by his own shield and that of the man on his right.

Soldiers on the far right are most vulnerable – so that's where a smart general will attack.

RUNNERS

Certain soldiers from Thrace called *peltasts* try a different tactic. They fire javelins into the phalanx to break it up, then pick off hoplites one by one. Younger, fitter hoplites known as *ekdromoi* are used to chase off these peltasts.

BACK IN THE SADDLE

As hoplites went from strength to strength, the role of the cavalry diminished. But soldiers on horseback will soon make a come back. Not only are they useful scouts, they're handy for breaking up an enemy phalanx.

UNDER SIEGE

A popular tactic is to lay siege to a city, surrounding it with an army and allowing no one in or out. The idea is to starve the city into submission – eventually. Of course the risk is that the army laying siege will also starve – or die of boredom.

A siege tower

An alternative is to storm the walls and a variety of weapons are available. (The following might look like a guide to medieval warfare, but the Greeks were there first.) Towers protect soldiers as they scale walls and, from the ground, catapults fire arrows and hurl rocks.

Then there's the ram. This is a huge tree trunk suspended on ropes and housed in a wooden case on wheels. It's rolled back and forth by soldiers.

Battering ram

In a variation on the ram, fire is sprayed on enemy buildings from a swinging cauldron.

Air is pumped down a hollow tree trunk to feed the fire.

THE NAVY

STICK YOUR OAR IN

The boats you'll be sailing rely on sails and the wind to propel them. This is no use in war. You can hardly say to an enemy commander, "Don't attack today. We're waiting for a decent wind." So, Greek warships have both sails and oars. At first, ships simply had a row of rowers, one down each side. But, since the more oarsmen you have, the faster you'll go, the latest addition to the Greek navy is the *trireme*, with three rows of oarsmen on each side.

THE TRIREME

A trireme's two great strengths are its speed and the fact that it's easy to steer. Assuming all oarsmen are rowing in sync, it's a quick job to start, stop or turn. They can row a boat into battle at up to 15km (9 miles) an hour – far faster than sails can ever manage. But triremes are not without drawbacks, being unsafe in storms and with limited space on board. Even so, they're the most successful and powerful warships in the Mediterranean.

A trireme

The prow (front) has a ram for sinking enemy ships.

Each oar is over 4m (14ft) long.

CAPTAIN & CREW

Triremes can carry a crew of up to 200 men, of whom all but 30 are rowers. The rest are officers, deckhands, archers and soldiers. Rowers sit in tiers (shown below). The crew is made up of professional sailors and free men, mostly recruited from the poorer classes.

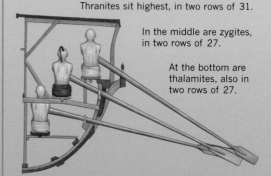

Thranites sit highest, in two rows of 31.

In the middle are zygites, in two rows of 27.

At the bottom are thalamites, also in two rows of 27.

The captain (*trierarch*) is a rich man chosen by the city to pay the ship's running costs for a year. He also usually pays someone else to go to sea in his place.

Wooden mast and linen sail

Sails and masts are lowered onto the deck before a battle.

Ships are steered from oars at the stern (back).

SEA WARFARE

At the start of most sea battles, the fleets face each other in two lines. Originally, oarsmen went all out, rowing as hard as they could, and rammed the enemy ship. If the ship didn't sink, at least it would be left in a bad way. Archers then fired arrows at the trapped enemy crew and soldiers went on board to finish them off in hand-to-hand combat.

The newest triremes, however, are light enough and fast enough for more daring tactics. A trireme's captain can now try to attack enemy ships from an unexpected angle – especially the sides and stern (back).

Four ways to sink a ship

1 Sweep around the line of enemy ships and attack from behind

2 Swerve in at the last moment, sweep past the enemy ship and break its oars

3 Swing to the side at the last moment, smashing into the enemy's side

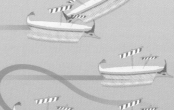

4 Dart through a gap in the line of ships, wheel around and attack from behind

A trireme caught in a storm

Triremes are much less stable when the mast and sails are up.

Steering the ship using an oar, which works like a rudder

Trierarch wishing he'd stayed at home

Captain

There's no room on board for cooking or sleeping facilities, so boats must land each night.

These oarsmen are shown clothed. Don't be shocked if you join a boat and find a crew of naked rowers.

GODS & GODDESSES

LEGENDARY LIVES

You won't get anywhere in Ancient Greece without some knowledge of the Immortals, the gods and goddesses who rule mortal lives. They're as familiar to the Greeks as their own families – and just as temperamental. Many stories are told to explain their personalities and let you know how to please (or avoid angering) them.

IN THE BEGINNING...

...*Gaea* (Mother Earth) arose out of chaos. She had a son, *Uranos* (Sky), whom she then married. They had dozens of children, including fourteen known as the Titans. One of these, *Cronos*, later deposed his father and married *Rhea*, his sister. (Different rules apply to the gods.)

Their youngest son, *Zeus*, followed family tradition, deposing his father and marrying his sister *Hera*. He led his brothers and sisters against their aunts and uncles, the Titans, and ruled from their new home on Mount Olympus. This earned them the nickname, the Olympians.

A WHO'S WHO OF GODS

Zeus: king of the gods, married to Hera. Theirs is a tempestuous relationship and he's had various flings with mortal women. His symbols are a thunderbolt, an eagle and an oak tree.

Hera: wife (and sister) of Zeus and protector of women and marriage. She's a beautiful but proud and jealous goddess, spending most of her time punishing the unfortunate mortals Zeus takes a fancy to. Her symbols are a cuckoo, a pomegranate and a peacock.

Poseidon: brother of Zeus and ruler of the sea. He lives in an underwater palace and is thought to cause earthquakes, hence his nickname, "Earthshaker". His symbols are a trident (three-pronged fork), dolphins and horses.

Hestia: goddess of the hearth and the most level-headed of the gods. There's a shrine to Hestia in every Greek home. She's gentle and pure, and keeps out of her relatives' constant quarrels.

Demeter: goddess of the plants, whose daughter Persephone was kidnapped by Pluto. Her search for Persephone led her to neglect the plants, causing winter. When Persephone returned, she brought spring and summer with her. Demeter's symbol is a sheaf of wheat or barley.

Ares: son of Zeus and Hera and god of war. He's young, strong and handsome but with a violent temper – not helped by the fact that he's constantly looking for a fight. His symbols are a burning torch, a spear, dogs and vultures.

Eris & Hebe: daughters of Zeus and Hera and very different sisters. Eris is goddess of spite – vengeful and troublesome – while Hebe is cupbearer to the gods.

Hephaestos: son of Zeus and Hera, he's a blacksmith whose forge stands beneath the volcanic Mount Etna on Sicily. He built his father's golden throne, and the shield which causes thunder and storms when shaken. He's the patron of craftsmen and husband of Aphrodite (not as great as it sounds).

Aphrodite: goddess of love and beauty, she may be married to Hephaestos but she's in love with Ares. Born in the sea, she rode to shore on a scallop shell. She's a real charmer, thanks largely to her golden belt which makes her irresistible. Her symbols are roses and doves, plus sparrows, dolphins and rams.

Artemis: the moon goddess, her silver arrows deliver plague and death, though she's a healer too. She protects young girls and pregnant women and, although she's mistress of wild animals, she's also a great hunter. Her symbols are cypress trees, deer and dogs.

Apollo: god of sun, light and truth and twin brother of Artemis. He's also the god to turn to for anything connected with music, poetry, science and healing. Apollo killed his mother's enemy, Python the serpent, when it took shelter in a shrine at Delphi. He then took over the shrine to be his oracle. His symbol is the laurel tree.

Hermes: as an impudent child and always up to mischief, he stole cattle from Apollo. But Apollo forgave him when Hermes gave him a lyre (a little like a guitar) he'd invented. To keep him out of trouble, Zeus made him the messenger of the gods. You might like to remember he's also the patron of tourists (and thieves). He wears wings on his hat and shoes, and carries a staff.

Dionysus: god of wine and fertility, he roams the countryside with his followers and gets to sit on Mount Olympus when Hestia leaves.

Athene: daughter of Zeus and Metis (a Titan). She sprang from Zeus's head fully armed. Goddess of wisdom and war, she is also, of course, the patron of Athens. Her symbols are an owl and an olive tree.

Pluto: ruler of the Underworld, the land of the dead. He guards his subjects jealously, rarely letting any return to the land of the living. He also owns all of the precious metals and gems on Earth.

Pluto in his chariot

Asclepius: son of Apollo, god of medicine and, if you believe the story, so good it killed him.

Asclepius learned medicine at the fetlock of his guardian, a centaur (half-man, half-horse). Athene then gave him two bottles of blood: one killed all it touched but the other revived the dead.

It meant that Asclepius cured one too many patients. Pluto told Zeus he was losing too many clients and Asclepius was killed. He was later made into a god by a guilty Zeus who was trying to make up.

DEATH & THE UNDERWORLD

THE FINAL JOURNEY

Greeks believe when they die their souls go to an underground world, only part of which is hell. Those who have led worthy lives end up in a place of happiness and eternal sunshine. They call this underworld Hades and believe it's ruled by Pluto.

FOUR STEPS TO PARADISE

Charon, the ferryman

2. You pay Charon, a ferryman, to take you across the river to the entrance of Hades. (If you haven't been buried with money, you'll be stuck on the bank forever.)

Hermes

1. Hermes, messenger of the gods, guides your soul to the River Styx, which divides the worlds of the living and the dead.

Cerberus

3. Skirt past Cerberus, the three-headed guard dog who keeps the living out and the dead in.

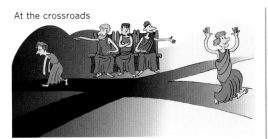
At the crossroads

4. Arrive at the crossroads of your death, where your life is judged. If you've been really good, you'll go on to the sunny Elysian Fields, to spend eternity singing, dancing and generally enjoying being dead.

THE ALTERNATIVES

Asphodel Fields

Those who haven't been especially good or bad end up in a boring place named the Asphodel Fields. (Imagine being grounded forever.)

Tartarus

But souls who have been wicked or cruel are sent to Tartarus, where they face being punished forever.

THE CHOSEN FEW

People who were part of a Mystery Cult have the option of rebirth. If they reach the Elysian Fields three times, they get to the Isle of the Blessed, a place of everlasting joy.

FUNERAL RITES

Getting the rites right is vital if the dead person is to reach Hades. First, the body is washed, doused in fragrant oils and dressed in white. Then it lies on display for people to pay their respects. Mourners wear black and women cut their hair as a sign of grief. On the day of the funeral, a coin is placed in the dead person's mouth to pay Charon, and the body is taken to its tomb, along with family, friends, musicians and professional mourners.

If you're out early, exploring, you may come across a funeral procession. Most set off before dawn for cemeteries outside the city. Don't be upset by the extreme emotions on display. This is a culture not afraid to show grief, with wailing, ripping of clothes and tearing of hair.

R.I.P.

Bodies are buried in the family plot or cremated. The rich are buried in elaborately carved stone coffins. Some even build tombs like small temples to hold them.

Tombs often display a stela, a portrait of the dead person.

FAMILY LIFE

A WOMAN'S PLACE

As you can't have failed to notice, women, particularly from the upper classes, are mostly stuck at home. A girl marries at fifteen, usually to a groom twice her age, taking money and goods from her dad to her new husband. This stays his unless they divorce, in which case wife, money and goods are sent back to Dad.

WEDDING BELLES

The day before her wedding, a girl burns her toys to show she's no longer a child. On the day itself, she dresses up and both families feast and make sacrifices – in their separate homes. The bride only goes to the groom's house that evening (in many cases, the first time they meet). It's only on the following day that families get together for feasting and presents.

TILL DIVORCE DO US PART

For a man to divorce his wife, he simply says as much in front of witnesses. For the woman it's much harder. She has to find an archon who agrees to act for her. In any event, she keeps only what she brought to the wedding from her father. And, whatever the situation, she must leave her children behind.

A WOMAN'S WORK

A Greek wife lives a similar life to a medieval lady in her castle. She looks after the children, stores and household finances; ensures the house is clean and that meals are on time and nurses sick family members. She also spends much of the day spinning and weaving the cloth that makes everyone's clothes.

ALL WORK & NO PLAY?

In some ways, the richer you are, the less fun you have. Wealthy women can only go to festivals and funerals – strictly chaperoned – or enjoy a rare dinner party with suitable female friends. Poorer women without slaves may have to shop and fetch water for themselves, but this gives them ample opportunities for a chat with friends in the market or by the public fountain.

MAD ABOUT THE BOY

In Ancient Greece, male babies are prized far above Rubies (or Helens or Jocastas). This is mainly because, as girls cannot earn money or own property, boys are more likely to support their aged parents. There are cases of fathers rejecting baby daughters and abandoning them. Some cities have specific places to leave unwanted babies, who are then brought up as slaves.

SCHOOLS & LEARNING

BOYS' SCHOOL

Since the purpose of education is to produce good citizens, only boys go to school. Girls are disqualified from citizenship by being girls. The luckier girls are taught at home by their mothers (assuming their mothers can read and write). All schools charge fees, so only boys with wealthy parents can attend.

3 SCHOOLS OF THOUGHT

Rather than learn everything at one school, boys go to a different school for separate subjects. At the first, a *grammatistes* teaches reading, writing and mathematics. The main difference you'll notice from today's classrooms is that instead of exercise books and calculators, boys use waxed boards and an abacus.

At the second school, boys learn poetry and music (including how to play the lyre and pipes), from a *kitharistes*. Dancing and athletics are taught by a *paidotribes*, who takes the boys to a *gymnasium* (training ground). Boys are usually accompanied to and from each school by a *paidagogos*. This paid chaperon keeps an eye on them during lessons too.

Boys start school at seven years old and continue to go until they're eighteen, when they begin military training. There's no higher education as such, but teachers known as *sophists* travel around teaching public speaking.

I HAVE AN IDEA!

If your heart sinks at the thought of a physics or history lesson, blame the Greeks. Not so long ago when people wanted answers to the eternal questions, they turned to the gods. But, from about the 6th century BC, Greek scholars have sought more practical explanations. They do this by closely observing the world around them. Their discoveries will form the basis of much that you learn in the 21st century.

Astronomy: an astronomer named Aristarchus has turned astronomy on its head by declaring that the Earth revolves around the Sun. Most Greeks believe the opposite.
History: the Persian Wars (shh! don't mention them) showed how useful it was to know all about your enemy. This has led to a mania for note-taking by the Greeks about their own lives and others.
Mathematics: new rules are being constantly introduced, including Pythagoras' theories on triangles and circles.
Physics: inspiration even strikes in the bathroom. Archimedes was taking a bath when he noticed that the water overflowed as he got in. Seeing this, he realized that an object displaces its own volume of liquid, enabling him to calculate an object's volume.

Archimedes taking a bath

CLOTHES & FASHION

A FOLD OF FABRIC

The key to Greek dress is simplicity: a rectangular piece of material draped over the body as a cloak or tunic. These cloth rectangles aren't due to a lack of imagination. It's simply that they're the easiest shape to produce on a loom. Wool or linen are used most often, though the rich splurge on silk or even cotton. (Cotton is expensive because it's imported from India.)

HIS...

In Ancient Greece it's the boys who get the chance to show off their legs (and tan). Young men choose either kilts or thigh-length tunics, leaving ankle-length tunics for the old and rich. Craftsmen and slaves wear even less, often just a loincloth. Many men, especially philosophers, also wear a *himation* (a rectangular wrap), either over their tunics or on its own. For travel or riding, the short cloak (*chlamys*) is popular.

Tunics are sewn up the sides and fastened on the shoulders.

The chlamys is fastened with a brooch.

The himation: simply wrap and go.

The younger you are, the higher your hem.

...AND HERS

Women wear a single, floor-length piece of cloth called a *chiton*. For those who like to vary their outfits, there's a choice of two: the *Doric* or the *Ionic*. Both are fastened with brooches or pins, and a belt is often worn around the waist. Women wear himations too, though theirs can be anything from a gauzy scarf to a full cloak.

Doric style: folded over at the top, then wrapped around the body with one side left open

Ionic style: fastened along the arms at intervals

Cloaked in a himation and ready to go out.

FASHION PARADE

Like everything, fashion goes in circles. Highly patterned tunics and clinging materials – recently a fashion no-no – are coming into their own again. To be at the forefront of this revival, wear bright, patterned tunics in the finest cloth you can afford. If money's no object, you can even find tunics with gold ornaments sewn into them.

FROM TOP...

Men have short hair and most have neatly-trimmed beards too. If you happen to pass a barber's shop, take a look at the shaving tackle. You'll see why most men steer clear of the clean-shaven option. In fact, even if you don't want a hair cut, male tourists should visit a barber's. It's where many men go simply to meet friends and catch up on local news.

Girls, of course, aren't allowed in, but most women grow their hair long anyway. It's always worn up and held in place with ribbons, scarves or nets. The only exceptions are slaves and women in mourning, whose hair is cut in a short bob. And, bad hair day or not, everyone wears hats outside to protect against the sun.

...TO TOE

Shoes are available, though most people opt to go barefoot. If the ground is too hot for your feet, you can pick up a pair of leather sandals at the market.

For a longer trip, and particularly if you're thinking of riding at some point, you might like to try a pair of calf-length boots for size. These are much sturdier than sandals, but far too hot to wear around the house.

COSTUME JEWELS

Both men and women wear decorative jewels of some sort: brooches, bracelets, necklaces, earrings or rings. There's something to suit every pocket too: gold, silver and ivory pieces for the rich; bronze, iron, lead, bone and glass for the poor. Each piece is elaborately carved and sometimes has enamel set into it. Precious stones, though, won't be used for some years.

Gold earring with a head also wearing earrings

COSMETICS

Greek women are as concerned about their appearance as 21st century girls, and you'll find a huge array of cosmetics and face creams on sale. Eager as you might be to experiment, you'd be wise to stick with toiletries from home. Not only are the creams and face packs for improving complexions unpleasantly smelly, the basic ingredient of face powder is the highly-toxic, powdered lead.

An unsuspecting Greek babe finishing herself off – literally – with toxic powder.

MYTHS & LEGENDS

BACK TO THE FUTURE

The Ancient Greeks are great storytellers, using tales of myth and magic to explain the often unbelievable world around them. Legends also tell the exploits of famous heroes in their history. Don't be surprised if some stories seem familiar. Even in the 21st century, writers look back to Ancient Greek tales for inspiration and plots.

PANDORA'S BOX

Zeus created the very first woman in the world out of clay and named her Pandora. He gave her a wonderful box, but forbade her to ever look inside. He must have known what would happen. One day, Pandora's curiosity got too much and she lifted the lid. Out flew all the bad things of the world: sins, sickness and death. But people weren't left in total despair, for there was one item left: Hope.

CHANGING SEASONS

Demeter, goddess of the harvest, had a beautiful daughter, Persephone. When Pluto, king of the Underworld, saw her he fell in love. But she refused to live in the Underworld, so he kidnapped her. Demeter was devastated and the crops went to ruin. Finally, Pluto agreed a compromise: he'd only keep Persephone for six months a year. When Persephone is with her mother, the sun shines and crops grow. But when autumn arrives, you know the reluctant Persephone is back with her hubby in Hades.

THESEUS & THE MINOTAUR

Once a year, 14 Athenians were sent to Crete to feed the Minotaur, a monstrous creature with the body of a man but the head of a bull. Theseus, a prince of Athens, decided it was time for the custom to stop. He set sail for Crete, swearing to return under white sails if he was successful. Theseus did manage to kill the Minotaur, escaping its maze-like lair using a ball of thread — thanks to an adoring princess who left Crete with him. But Theseus then dumped the princess on an island. To punish him, the gods made him forget his promise, and he sailed home under black sails. His father, Aegeus, thinking Theseus was dead, threw himself off a cliff in despair and was drowned.

PERSEUS & THE GORGON

Perseus, a son of Zeus, was told to kill Medusa, a fearsome gorgon. Not only did she have snakes where other people have hair, her glance turned men to stone. The goddess Athene gave Perseus a mirror so he didn't have to look directly into the gorgon's deadly eyes. Thus, Perseus managed to kill Medusa and gave her terrible head to Athene, who stuck it on her shield. (Which shows that, even where gods are concerned, there's no accounting for taste.)

ANCIENT ROME

ABOUT ROME

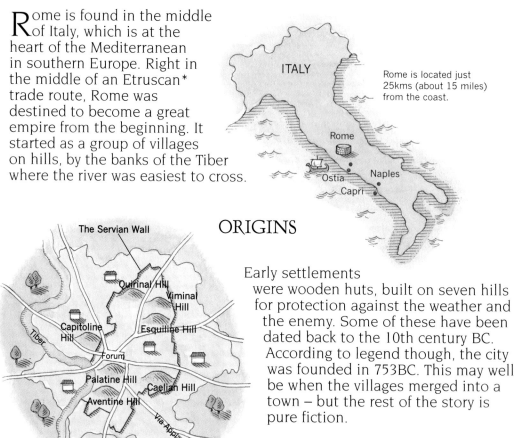

Rome is found in the middle of Italy, which is at the heart of the Mediterranean in southern Europe. Right in the middle of an Etruscan* trade route, Rome was destined to become a great empire from the beginning. It started as a group of villages on hills, by the banks of the Tiber where the river was easiest to cross.

ITALY

Rome is located just 25kms (about 15 miles) from the coast.

Rome

Ostia · Naples

Capri

ORIGINS

Early settlements were wooden huts, built on seven hills for protection against the weather and the enemy. Some of these have been dated back to the 10th century BC. According to legend though, the city was founded in 753BC. This may well be when the villages merged into a town – but the rest of the story is pure fiction.

The Servian Wall

Quirinal Hill

Viminal Hill

Capitoline Hill

Esquiline Hill

Tiber

Forum

Palatine Hill

Caelian Hill

Aventine Hill

Via Appia

The "Seven Hills" of Rome, surrounded by the Servian Wall, which enclosed the early city

ONCE UPON A TIME...

... twin boys called Romulus and Remus were cast into the Tiber by a wicked uncle, who had murdered their grandfather and stolen his throne. The boys drifted to a marshy area under the Capitoline Hill, where they were washed ashore and suckled by a she-wolf.

Years later, Mars (the God of War) told them to build a city where they'd been abandoned. But, during the founding ceremony, Remus ridiculed the boundary wall. In a rage, Romulus killed him, and became the sole ruler of the city he named Rome.

This bronze statue of a she-wolf may be Etruscan. Romulus and Remus are later additions.

* The Etruscans lived in northwest Italy and had a thriving civilization before the Romans.

STRUCTURE OF SOCIETY

Before you spend time in Rome, it's useful to know a little about Roman society. This consists of two groups: citizens, called *cives*, and non-citizens. Eligibility for citizenship has varied over the years. Originally, a man (women don't count) had to be born in Rome of Roman parents. Later, anyone (male) thought worthy could become a citizen.

CITIZENS

Within the rank of citizen there are three divisions:

Patricians: the richest and the ruling class

Equites: the businessmen and bankers

Plebeians (commoners): the poorest

NON-CITIZENS

Non-citizens are divided into:

Provincials: people living in the Roman Empire, who must pay taxes

Foreigners: everyone who lives outside the Roman Empire

Slaves: owned by other people and bought and sold like property

CITIZENS OF ROME...

In recent times, especially under Hadrian, citizenship has been extended to people all the way across the empire. Being a citizen is no bad thing – they enjoy numerous privileges not open to others, including voting in elections. They don't pay the same taxes as the provincials either, though they do have the dubious right to serve in the army.

To carry off temporary citizenship, see the tip below:

TOP TIPS FOR TOURISTS
No. 2: Toga!

Only citizens are allowed to wear the traditional Roman toga. If you plan on convincing the natives you're a citizen too, buy one as soon as possible.

ARRIVING

Everyone's first impressions are different but, as you arrive, several things will hit you in the face. There's the heat, the noise, crowded streets with no cars, and the overpowering smell of food being cooked. On top of that, everyone will be speaking in Latin. After taking a few minutes to accustom yourself to your new surroundings, take the plunge. The first thing you'll need to organize is somewhere to stay.

WHERE TO STAY

A lthough Rome has tens of thousands of visitors a year, their expectations are probably much lower than yours. Modern day tourists are likely to find Rome's inns less than satisfactory. Some aren't respectable, or even clean. Facilities will be basic and the atmosphere rowdy, to say the least.

RENTING

Your best bet is to try to rent somewhere – an apartment in an *insula* (block) if money's tight; a *domus* (town house) if you're feeling rich. Many wealthy Romans move out to country villas during the summer, which should help your search. But bear in mind that, if you want a *domus*, there are only 2,000 in all of Rome, whereas there are more than 47,000 *insulae**.

The higher you go, the more crowded the apartment block. With rent so high, Romans rent out rooms to other families.

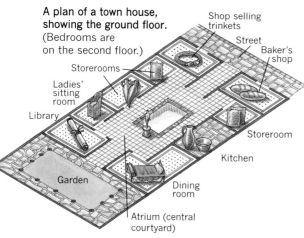

A plan of a town house, showing the ground floor. (Bedrooms are on the second floor.)

- Shop selling trinkets
- Street
- Baker's shop
- Storerooms
- Ladies' sitting room
- Library
- Storeroom
- Kitchen
- Garden
- Dining room
- Atrium (central courtyard)

Best of all, you might be able to find an apartment belonging to a government official working in one of Rome's provinces. In that case, the flat will not only be furnished, but a cook and household staff will probably be included in the rent.

Expect to fork out a fair amount wherever you stay: buying a country estate costs the same as a year's rent on an apartment in Rome. If you do settle for an apartment, go for smaller buildings: nothing over four floors. They have fewer (noisy) tenants, are better built, and less of a fire risk.

Avoid places with shops on the ground floor and go for a ground floor apartment – these often have a kitchen and water supply. Pick one away from the markets, or the noise of carts being unloaded will keep you awake all night. (Most wheeled vehicles are only allowed to enter the city between sunset and dawn.)

* Insulae is the plural of insula.

Communal lavatories are situated on the ground floor of some apartment buildings. They're considered sociable places to meet and chat.

FEW AMENITIES

Luxury apartments have running water and even bathrooms, but most are mainly a place to sleep. To bathe, everyone goes to the public baths (pages 130-133); for food, they visit one of the plethora of eating places Rome has to offer (pages 126-129). Lavatories are also public, charging a nominal 1 *as* (see page 174).

SANITATION

The city's system of drainage is second to none. Seven sewers underground wash waste into the Tiber river via the massive *Cloaca Maxima* (Great Drain). This sewer, a natural waterway, was developed into a canal system by the Etruscans.

FREE-FLOWING WATER

Rome has an unrivalled water supply in the form of 10 channels, or aqueducts, which carry a constant torrent of fresh water into the city. The penalty for blocking it is severe – a fine of up to 10,000 *sestertii*.

Water

Aqueducts supply water for the public baths, fountains and lavatories.

TOP TIPS FOR TOURISTS
No. 3: Air freshener

Before you agree to rent anywhere, check that the landlord, or his agent, arranges for the stairs and hallways to be regularly swept and cleaned. Your rooms will still get stuffy, though. Pliny (a Roman writer and senator) burns bread in his rooms to counteract this. If you prefer the smell of charred toast to sweat, you might like to try it.

EATING & DRINKING

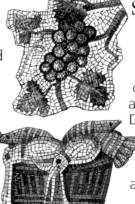

R ome is bursting with
taverns and market
stalls, providing hot and
cold snacks and cooked food
to eat in or take home. This
is one example of where an
essential drawback – the
fact that most apartments
don't have kitchens
because of the fire risk –
works to the advantage
of the hungry tourist.

SNACK BARS

Many people eat in the street,
though most snack bars have
somewhere you can sit down.
Even the fussiest eater
should find food he
recognizes, from bread
and cheese to hot pies,
sausages, bacon and beans,
or fried fish. As a general
guide, check that the
snack bar is clean and
the dishes aren't
swimming in olive oil.

SALADS AND SWEETS

For the health conscious,
there's a wide variety of
salad and vegetable dishes
on offer, though vegetables
are often fried or roasted.
Desserts include pastries and
honeycakes. There are
also endless amounts of
fresh fruit: melons, grapes,
apples, figs, plums and pears.

THE MAIN MEAL

If the Romans bother with
breakfast, it's a snack of
wheat biscuits dipped in
honey. Lunch can be light,
perhaps bread and cheese,
though some enjoy salads,
eggs and cold meats. It's
dinner which is the main meal
of the day (see pages 128-129).

Pictures showing the food on offer are displayed on the walls
outside snack bars. There are no menus – so even if your Latin
is rusty, you won't order fried cow's udders by mistake.

Eating in the street, you
can use your fingers,
though most
Romans carry
their own knife
and spoon
with them.

Food is stored
in covered jars,
held in holes in
the counter to
keep warm.

TOP TIPS FOR TOURISTS
No. 4: Self-catering

If you get fed-up with eating out, you could buy and prepare your own food. Officially, most apartments don't have kitchens, but the previous tenants may have set up an illegal brick stove. These rest on wooden floors, so be careful not to start a fire.

Public bakeries will cook a prepared meal for you, but they charge, which is why there are so many illegal stoves and so many outbreaks of fire.

SEASONING

Whatever you eat, you'll find it strongly seasoned. Chefs use herbs and spices liberally, and douse most dishes in sauce. One of the most popular is the salty fish pickle sauce, *liquamen*. Be careful if you have a delicate stomach: it's very strong. (One version contains fish entrails which have been left to rot in a pot of brine for six weeks.)

Honey is used as a sweetener, not only for desserts but also with meat and fish. Concentrated wine and dried raisins are also used to enhance a dish's taste. Sugar is very expensive as it comes from India. It's never used in cooking, though it is found in some medicines.

DAILY BREAD

Bread is a staple part of the Roman diet and loaves come in a selection of sizes. You can buy them plain or with added seeds, nuts, herbs or spices. Each baker puts in his own unique blend of ingredients. Look for the distinctive pattern or mark on some loaves. Just like famous brand names, several bakers have their own mark to encourage customers to return to them.

DRINKING

Wine, often spiced or sweetened with honey and generally watered down, is on sale everywhere. There are almost 200 varieties to choose from. If you'd rather have a soft drink, you can buy grape juice or honey-sweetened water. There are also dozens of public drinking fountains, continually supplied with water carried in from aqueducts outside Rome.

This might look like a fancy sculpture, but it's a typical Roman drinking fountain.

THE EVENING MEAL

Dinner, or *cena*, the main meal of the day, used to be eaten as early as two-thirty in the afternoon. It's now held in the early evening, customarily after a visit to the baths. Despite the stories, not all Romans gorge themselves on lavish banquets. Many eat much plainer meals of roast poultry or fish with vegetables, followed by fresh fruit. As for the poor and slaves, they make do with wheat porridge or a vegetable stew of peas, beans and lentils.

FEASTING FIT TO BUST

If you are invited to a banquet, leap at the chance. It's worth trying once, just for the experience. At the door, you'll be announced by a *nomenclator* (usher). Be ready to take off your sandals. Your feet must be washed by a slave before you can enter the *triclinium* (dining room). The usher will then show you to your place and a slave will come to wash your hands before the meal begins.

You may be served flamingo tongues or sow's udders with sea urchins.

Acrobats and musicians are usually on hand to amuse diners. If you're unlucky, your host will read you his poetry.

One side of the table is clear of couches for the slaves to serve from. The couch opposite seats the most important guests.

Nine is the maximum number of guests around a table.

TOP TIPS FOR TOURISTS
No. 5: Table napkins

Each diner spreads a napkin in front of him to protect the host's couch. It's a good idea to bring your own. Then you can use it to take away any leftover food.

"Seating", or rather "lying", is arranged in order of the guests' importance. All guests recline on mattresses spread with cushions. Don't ask for a chair – only slaves and young children sit to eat.

Tiny spoons are provided to eat the egg and shellfish starters.

TABLE MANNERS

Although knives and spoons are available, most people eat with their fingers. Forks are completely unheard of. Food is generally cut up before it leaves the kitchen, but eating is still a messy business. After each course, slaves will pour perfumed water over your hands and wipe them dry. Elegant toothpicks will also be offered.

Don't be surprised by the antics of fellow-diners. Not only do they spit, they show their appreciation of a meal by burping. You might try out a few rounded belches beforehand. Not burping risks insulting your host. Just remember to break the habit back home.

ON THE MENU

Arrive hungry: seven courses are the norm. You'll begin simply, with various cold dishes. After a sip of *mulsum* (honey wine), the menu gets really exotic. Most dishes are good but, even though everyone else will pile their plates high, you'd be wise to try small portions first. And don't forget to leave room for dessert. You'll probably only want one pastry though – they're sickeningly sweet.

Certain households are known for "unusual" cuisine. Be warned: these dishes can taste truly disgusting. Roman cooks pride themselves on their ability to disguise food, so pork may look like fish or duck. In extreme cases, not recognizing what you are eating is not a bad thing.

TABLE TALK

To break the ice, compliment your host on his tablecloth if he has one. They're the latest fad, so he probably will. You'll find conversation focuses on local gossip rather than more elevated topics, and fellow guests may seem sarcastic, even blunt. Avoid arguments such as whether the Earth is round. Though the Greeks have long since discovered this, some Romans still can't believe it.

There'll also be plenty of entertainment from the hired acts – musicians and dancers, even conjurors – to provide a welcome break between courses.

MENU

Gustatio (starter)
A selection of radishes, lettuce, eggs, mushrooms, oysters, cheese and sardines

Mulsum

Entrées
Fried mullet with prawns
Mackerel in a tuna fish sauce
served with hot rolls

Roasts
Roast venison with leeks fried in honey
Roast boar in liquamen sauce
served with cabbage, turnips,
beans and peas

Secundae mensae (dessert)
Honey cakes, stuffed dates, fresh fruit,
including apples, pears and grapes,
figs and nuts

BATHING

Rome has 11 public baths or *thermae* which are open to all and are far more than just places to bathe (see next pages). The tiled floors are probably the only thing they'll have in common with your local pool, unless that has marble pillars, high, domed ceilings and statues in every corner.

There are also several privately owned baths in Rome. These are more exclusive, offering greater privacy and sometimes special attractions such as celebrity masseurs, but they are strictly for the wealthy.

OPENING HOURS

Most public baths open around mid-morning and close at sunset. For privacy, men and women are admitted to the bathing areas at separate times of day – women in the morning, men in the afternoon.

Although in Nero's time mixed bathing was encouraged, this is strictly a thing of the past. Steer clear of baths offering mixed facilities. They're not respectable!

SOAP ON A STICK?

You can't buy soap, but there are plentiful supplies of oil, which the Romans use instead. This is smeared over your body, then scraped off (along with the grime), with a curved stick called a *strigil*.

Strigils can be rented at the baths, but they're very cheap to buy. It's probably a good idea to buy your own from a market (see pages 158-159), especially if you plan to visit the baths regularly during your stay.

They're tricky to use on your own, though. Hold the bumpy end and scrape the curved part over your skin. If you can afford it, hire an attendant to scrape you off – but be warned, their services aren't cheap. The next best thing is to go with a friend and scrape each other.

A metal strigil – strigils can also be made of wood or bone. They're often carried on a ring like keys, with a scoop for pouring oil.

TOP TIPS FOR TOURISTS
No. 6: Changing rooms

If your household doesn't have a slave, hire someone at the baths to keep an eye on your things. The changing rooms don't have lockers, just unguarded shelves where everyone leaves their clothes, and thefts are common.

ENTRANCE FEES

Charges are a nominal *quadrans* for men. Women can pay more (up to an *as*) but for a full day's admission, including facilities, it's worth it. If money's tight, the **Baths of Agrippa** are free, and children get in free to all the baths in Rome. Wealthy citizens seeking election often pay everyone's fees for the day too.

GUIDE TO THE BATHS

The baths are made up of several rooms, customarily visited in a specific order. To get into the spirit of the thing, you can visit the on-site gym first for some weight-lifting or wrestling. If that's too energetic for you, head straight for the *apodyterium* (changing room) where you leave your clothes. The plan below gives the layout of a typical bathhouse, showing the rooms and the order you visit them.

WARNING!
Not everyone wants to see a guidebook with naked figures, so we've covered the bathers in our pictures with towels. At the baths, however, nudity is not just accepted but expected.

3 The caldarium, almost as hot as the laconicum, has a hot pool. It's often housed in a rotunda (a domed room). This is where you use your strigil.

2 The *sudatorium*, or *laconicum*, is a hot air bath like a sauna. Hot air runs under the floor and inside the walls, so you'll work up a good sweat.

Massage room

1 The apodyterium or changing room has no cubicles.

4 The tepidarium is a large vaulted hall with a gently-warmed (or tepid) pool. Here, you can gradually cool off as you bathe.

5 The final bath is the frigidarium, an unheated, open-air swimming pool.

WATER PALACES

op of any tourist's "must-see" list are Trajan's Baths, the biggest Rome has to offer and catering for up to 10,000 people at a time. They've been open for eight years and were inaugurated on June 22nd 109AD, the same day as Trajan's aqueduct, the *Aqua Trajana*.

The baths are palatial, with marble walls and pillars, and domed ceilings high above. Many of the ceilings have central holes which let in light. On a bright day, sunlight streams through, heating the rooms.

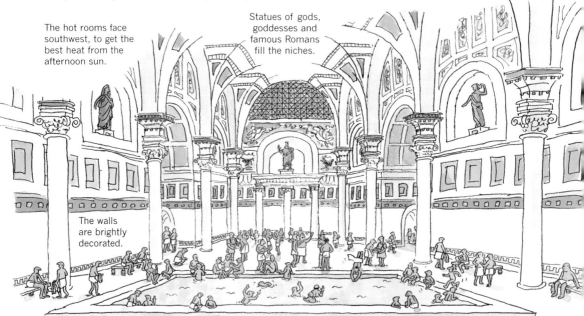

The hot rooms face southwest, to get the best heat from the afternoon sun.

Statues of gods, goddesses and famous Romans fill the niches.

The walls are brightly decorated.

Baths are as much a chance to socialize as to get clean.

The baths took five years to put up, on a giant platform built into the hillside. There are entrances on all sides, but to appreciate their magnificence fully, on your first visit go in through the grand entrance on the northeast side.

Niches filled with amazing statues line every wall. The statue to look out for is the **Laocoön Group**. This magnificent sculpture shows Laocoön, who was the priest of the god Apollo, and his two sons being attacked by serpents.

TOP TIPS FOR TOURISTS
No. 7: The roar of the crowd

Trajan's Baths are certainly the finest, but with anything up to several thousand visitors at a time, they can get very crowded, not to mention noisy. If you prefer to bathe in peace, try the **Baths of Titus** nearby (opposite the Colosseum). They're older and the facilities are less grand, but they're much more restful.

PIPING HOT WATER

In the basement, you can see how the baths are heated. The Romans have invented the *hypocaust*, the first underfloor central heating. But go first thing; it gets unbearably hot. Any later and you'll be dodging fainting slaves, collapsing as they stoke the fires which heat the rooms.

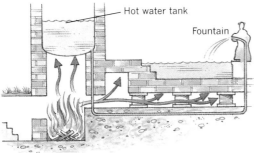

Hot air circulates through tunnels under the baths.

THE TRAJAN CISTERN

It may be a humble cistern (water container), but it's a prime example of Roman engineering. Set into a hill next to the baths, the cistern distributes water to all parts of the bath building. It holds an amazing 8,000,000l (just over 2,000,000 gals) of water stored on two levels, flowing in from the Julian and Claudian aqueducts.

FUN AND GAMES

Next to cleanliness, in the Roman mind at least, is healthiness, and all baths have gyms and playing grounds attached. Here, you can join in a variety of games, including a form of tennis using your hands instead of a racket.

Games counters and dice for those who prefer less energetic games

Harpastum, named after its sand-filled ball, is a more aggressive ball game. The aim is to get the ball from the other players. Shoving isn't against the rules: it's a good tactic.

Trigon is a game with less contact. Players stand one at each corner of a triangle, throwing balls back and forth at each other without warning. It calls for concentration – you throw and catch simultaneously.

REST AND RELAX!

If running around is just too active for you, don't worry. The baths are surrounded with everything you need for more leisurely pursuits.

A bone comb, a spatula for applying cosmetics, and a flask of cream for beauty treatments after a bath

As well as playing grounds, there are libraries, exhibition halls, covered walkways with fountains, and landscaped gardens. You can have a snack, enjoy a massage, visit a barber, go for a stroll – or all four if the mood takes you. And if being on vacation really takes hold and you feel like a change, you can treat yourself to a Roman makeover by a beautician.

OUT AND ABOUT

As you'd expect in a city of its size, Rome is fast becoming grid-locked. In fact, wheeled vehicles have been banned from the city between dawn and dusk since Caesar's time. This means that most of your visiting will be done on foot.

This wouldn't be a problem if the streets were pleasant places to walk. Certainly, the major streets are swept clean, though they're often unbearably crowded. But in smaller streets and alleys, you'll be up to the ankles in garbage, and even sewage. You'll also be a prime target for any itinerant beggar who happens to cross your path.

The streets are paved, though, and most sights are fairly close together, so walking isn't such a bad option – as long as you watch your step. You certainly get the feel of the city this way. But be careful crossing roads: the wheels of the night-time traffic wear deep grooves in them, which fill with rainwater.

HIRING A "CAB"

The alternative to pedestrian sightseeing is to hire a litter. This is a wheel-less carriage used by the wealthier citizens and carried by slaves. Choose carefully. They range from the luxurious, with padded cushions, to the dirty, greasy and falling apart.

Being carried in a litter can often prove to be a bumpy ride.

ROMAN UFOs?

Watch out for falling masonry if you decide to walk. The Romans' feats of engineering are second to none, but they also have "cowboy" builders who want a quick profit, no matter how shakily an apartment block is put up.

A typical street scene in the city: apartments are built close together, to cram in as many as possible.

Handcarts are one way of getting around the ban on wheeled vehicles.

Soldiers herding prisoners-of-war are a common sight.

A water carrier

A water trough

A ball game

NO-GO AREAS

Even if you want to see the seedier side of Roman life (and it's not all banquets and mosaics), avoid the **Subura** area. It's a slum, the home of Rome's poorest inhabitants and the most disreputable area in Rome. Inevitably, it's become the haunt of thieves, who prey on the unwary.

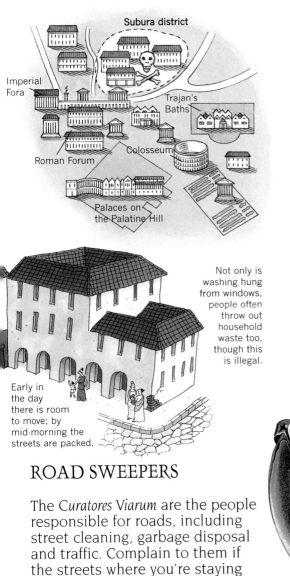

Subura district

Imperial Fora

Trajan's Baths

Roman Forum

Colosseum

Palaces on the Palatine Hill

Not only is washing hung from windows, people often throw out household waste too, though this is illegal.

Early in the day there is room to move; by mid-morning the streets are packed.

ROAD SWEEPERS

The *Curatores Viarum* are the people responsible for roads, including street cleaning, garbage disposal and traffic. Complain to them if the streets where you're staying get in too much of a mess.

GETTING LOST

If you do get lost, don't panic. Keep your head and look for a familiar sight with which to orientate yourself. If you should find yourself in the **Subura** district, however, GET OUT AS FAST AS YOU CAN!

TAKE A TORCH

As darkness descends, the already crowded city becomes a nightmare scenario when wheeled vehicles are let in. With no street lighting, most Romans head straight for home. You should too. Hire a torchbearer to guide you safely through the unlit streets. Squads of night watchmen patrol the city, but there aren't enough for every part of town.

TOP TIPS FOR TOURISTS
No. 8: Keep a pocket watch

Like all cities, Rome is full of thieves or "cutpurses". If you don't have a money belt, buy a draw-string purse. Hide it in the folds of your toga though, or the strings will be cut, hence the expression "cutpurses". Hard to come by, but more effective, is a soldier's wrist purse, shown below.

Purses like this can only be opened once they've been taken off.

GETTING SICK

It happens to nearly everyone on vacation, sooner or later: you have an accident or become sick. There's no shortage of Roman treatments if the worst happens, from chanting to eating dung. But more effective, or at least preferable, is to consult a doctor.

Many doctors work from shops which are open to the road. If you value your privacy, look for one who has rooms in a *domus*. But be warned: there's no formal system of training. Doctors start as apprentices and learn by watching doctors already in practice. There are no qualifications either: in Rome, anyone can call himself a doctor. To be absolutely safe, unless you're desperate, go home for treatment.

REMEDIES

Medicines are made from plants, particularly herbs, and minerals. (There are reputedly as many as 42 remedies made from lettuce alone.) Plants are crushed with a pestle and mortar and made into pills, or added to wine to make a linctus. Doctors don't just prescribe pills though. They're as likely to advise you on the importance of a healthy diet, fresh air and exercise.

Radishes are among the more unusual "drugs". You might decide to skip the doctor and eat a large salad instead.

MEDICINE AND RELIGION

Although Roman medicine is based to some extent on observation and scientific fact (which comes mainly from the writings of Greek doctors), it's also closely tied up with religion. The causes of disease are barely understood – your doctor is likely to blame your illness on a curse. Most Romans, their doctors included, believe the gods can cure people. A common response to illness is to sleep in the temple of Asclepius, god of medicine, in the hope of dreaming a cure. If a particular part of your body troubles you, leave a small model of it (a votive) in the temple. It will remind Asclepius which part of you needs healing.

A votive eye

66 *I was sick so the Doctor hurried over – with ninety students. Ninety cold hands prodded me. I wasn't well before; now I'm really sick.* 99

Martial (see page 185)

OPTICIANS

The only opticians are actually doctors who specialize in eye complaints. You certainly won't be able to get a sight test, or replace a broken pair of glasses. If you come down with an eye infection though, there are various ointments on offer, and – in extreme cases – even cataract operations are performed.

A hook to hold open
wounds during operations

SURGERY

Tweezers

Many doctors are better
at surgery than curing
illnesses, especially
the ones who trained in
army hospitals. They
have vast experience of
anatomy and surgery
from treating the
wounds of hundreds of
soldiers. Operations
can be quite complex,
from setting broken
bones to amputating
limbs, though these
shouldn't be necessary
unless you're very
accident-prone.

Surgeons have a wide
range of bronze and
iron instruments at
their disposal,
some very delicate.
But despite their
equipment and expertise,
operations are highly
dangerous. With no
anesthetics or painkillers,
even patients who survive
an operation are likely to
die of shock or infection
soon after.

DENTISTS

If you have a toothache during your
stay, you'll be able to find a dentist,
but you may not like the treatment.
Fillings are unheard of. Instead,
your bad teeth will be extracted and
false teeth offered in replacement.

Teeth are fixed to a
gold band which
won't rust.

TOP TIPS FOR TOURISTS
No. 9: No insurance?

Don't panic if money's short
and you can't afford
consultation fees. A state health
system has recently been
introduced. Doctors who are
part of the scheme aren't taxed
on their earnings from richer
patients, provided they treat the
poorest patients for free.

Here, an apprentice
medic is given the chance
to put his knowledge into
practice.

Mixing herbs with a pestle
and mortar.

Jugs of wine – the
only option for
dulling pain

Without X-rays, doctors have
to diagnose by feel.

THE ROMAN FORUM

There's a forum at the heart of every Roman town. Part market-place, part law court, part religious district, part political arena, it's the place to go for the latest gossip. Each forum usually follows the same basic layout: three covered walkways for offices and shops, making three sides of a square, with the *basilica* or law court forming the fourth. The *curia* (senate house), temples and shrines stand within the square.

The first to be built, however, was the **Roman Forum**, which doesn't follow this pattern. In fact, so many shrines and statues were added, it became too crowded for people to meet. So successive emperors, beginning with Caesar, built their own *fora** – the **Imperial Fora** – alongside (see pages 140-141). But it's in the Roman Forum that you'll really begin to appreciate the majesty and grandeur of Rome.

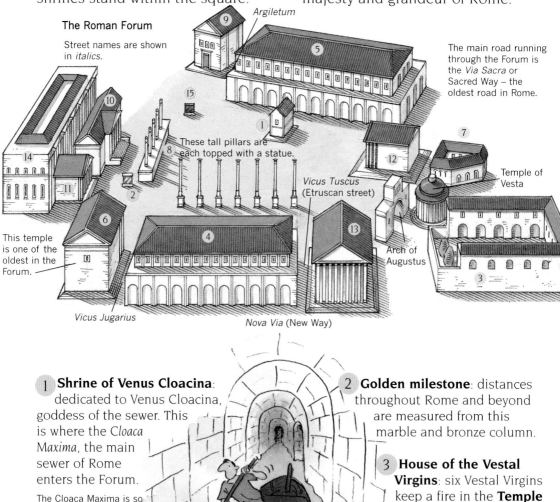

The Roman Forum

Street names are shown in *italics*.

Argiletum

The main road running through the Forum is the *Via Sacra* or Sacred Way – the oldest road in Rome.

These tall pillars are each topped with a statue.

Vicus Tuscus (Etruscan street)

Temple of Vesta

This temple is one of the oldest in the Forum.

Arch of Augustus

Vicus Jugarius

Nova Via (New Way)

1 **Shrine of Venus Cloacina**: dedicated to Venus Cloacina, goddess of the sewer. This is where the *Cloaca Maxima*, the main sewer of Rome enters the Forum.

The Cloaca Maxima is so large in places, it would be possible to sail a boat through it – not that you'd want to...

2 **Golden milestone**: distances throughout Rome and beyond are measured from this marble and bronze column.

3 **House of the Vestal Virgins**: six Vestal Virgins keep a fire in the **Temple of Vesta** constantly alight. If it goes out, legend says disaster will befall Rome.

*Fora is the Latin plural of forum.

Lawyers hire crowds to cheer them on and boo their opponents, so trials can get rowdy.

4 **Basilica Julia**: a court house, begun by Julius Caesar, the Republican dictator, in around 55BC. 180 magistrates try cases here. If you have a spare half hour, sit in on a trial in the public gallery upstairs.

5 **Basilica Aemilia**: the second basilica or law court to be built in Rome, it was put up in 179BC.

6 **Temple of Saturn**: the first temple to the god Saturn on this site dates back to the beginning of the Republic*, some 500-600 years ago. Saturn was said to have taught the Romans how to farm.

In December, the lively festival of Saturnalia is held. Masters and slaves switch places for the day and gifts are exchanged.

7 **Regia**: the official headquarters of the chief priest of Rome.

8 **Rostra**: the large stone platform initially used by public speakers to rouse the crowds. Now it's mostly used for official ceremonies. The name comes from the ships' *rostra* (prows) which decorate it.

9 **Curia** (Senate House): during the Republic, senators met here to govern Rome. Before each session, the President would consult an *augur* (someone who interprets messages from the gods). Though they still meet, senators now have little sway: emperors are all-powerful.

An augur, usually a senator, is a highly respected religious figure.

10 **Temple of Concord** (Peace): built to celebrate the peace between warring factions in Rome in the third century BC.

11 **Temple of Vespasian**: a temple built in memory of the emperor Vespasian. (Emperors become gods after they die.)

12 **Temple of Caesar**: dedicated to Julius Caesar and built on the spot where his body was cremated. Inside, is a statue of Caesar with a star on his head. This is because a comet appeared during the weeks of shows given by Augustus in Caesar's memory.

Many people believe the comet was Caesar's soul going up to heaven.

13 **Temple of Castor**: dedicated to the god Jupiter's twin sons, Castor and Pollux, who are said to have helped the Romans in battle.

14 **Tabularium**: the public record office, where state records are kept.

15 **Lapis Niger** (Black stone): a slab of black marble which some say marks the grave of Romulus, founder of Rome. Others think it is the site of an old temple to the god Vulcan.

* See page 188

139

THE IMPERIAL FORA

The first of the five **Imperial Fora** was begun by Caesar in 51BC, when the Roman Forum became too small to hold the crowds who gathered to discuss politics, attend court or simply to trade. Augustus, Vespasian, Nerva and Trajan then added their fora alongside. Like the original, all contain law courts, shops, markets and temples.

Plan of the Imperial Fora
(The original Roman Forum is just to the left of Caesar's Forum.)

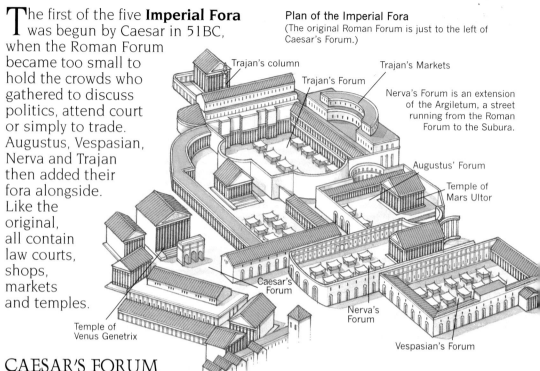

- Trajan's column
- Trajan's Forum
- Trajan's Markets
- Nerva's Forum is an extension of the Argiletum, a street running from the Roman Forum to the Subura.
- Augustus' Forum
- Temple of Mars Ultor
- Caesar's Forum
- Nerva's Forum
- Vespasian's Forum
- Temple of Venus Genetrix

CAESAR'S FORUM

To make room for his forum, Caesar had to buy and demolish an entire street of houses which stood in the way. Costs are estimated at between 60 million and 100 million sestertii. You can judge for yourself whether it was worth it. Caesar's Forum was partly damaged in a fire in AD80, but Domitian began restoration work, which Trajan has just completed.

You can reach **Caesar's Forum** via the Curia in the Roman Forum. Dominating the scene is the **Temple of Venus Genetrix**, from whom Caesar claimed he was descended.

In front of the temple is a statue of Caesar on his horse, displaying its unusual hooves. (Soothsayers are said to have told Caesar that the split hooves were a sign from the gods that he would rule the world.) Inside is a statue of Venus, based on the Egyptian queen, Cleopatra.

Close by is the **Tullianum**, a prison which houses enemies of the state. It consists of two underground rooms, cut out of the Capitoline Hill. Legend has it that Saint Peter and Saint Paul were imprisoned here.

Saint Peter is said to have made water flow from the earth to baptize guards and inmates.

FORA GALORE

Vespasian's Forum is also known as the Peace Forum. A Temple of Peace was built here in AD71, after the Jews were defeated in a war in Judea (Palestine).

Augustus' Forum stretches from the Roman Forum up to a slum district. The back wall is high, to keep the forum apart from the hovels behind it, and to protect it from the frequent fires which rage through them. This forum has the **Temple of Mars Ultor**, which is now a museum for relics, including Caesar's sword.

Trajan's Forum is overlooked by his magnificent markets (see pages 158-159) and consists of a basilica, a temple, and a courtyard with two libraries, one on either side of his famous column.

TRAJAN'S COLUMN

Trajan's Column, 38m (125ft) high, is made up of marble panels going up in a spiral. The panels show episodes from wars Trajan waged – over 100 scenes are illustrated. As the column goes higher, its width increases, so it doesn't look as if it narrows at the top. The panels are larger too. In a chamber at the base is a golden urn containing the ashes of Trajan and his wife – the only Romans allowed to be buried within the city.

TOP TIPS FOR TOURISTS
No. 10: Trajan's Column

For the best view of this stunning sculpture, head for the roof-top terrace on one of the Forum's libraries.

A detail from Trajan's column showing shipbuilders at work

ANCIENT ROME: MAIN SIGHTS

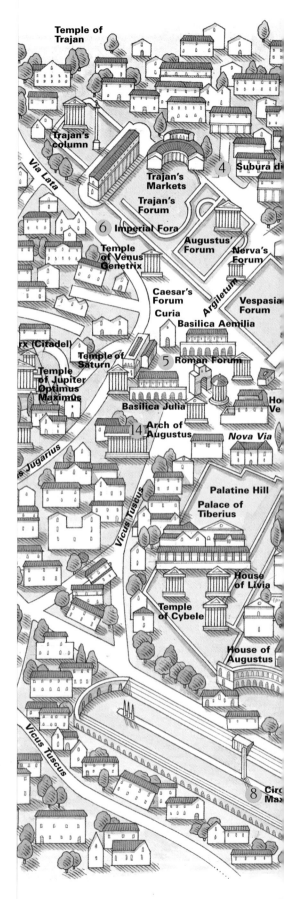

Temple of
Trajan

Via Lata

Trajan's
column

4 Subura di

Trajan's
Markets

Trajan's
Forum

6 Imperial Fora

Augustus'
Forum

Nerva's
Forum

Temple
of Venus
Genetrix

Caesar's
Forum

Argiletum

Vespasia
Forum

Curia

rx (Citadel)

Basilica Aemilia

Temple of
Saturn

5 Roman Forum

Temple
of Jupiter
Optimus
Maximus

Basilica Julia

Ho
Ve

s Jugarius

14 Arch of
Augustus

Nova Via

Vicus Tuscus

Palatine Hill

Palace of
Tiberius

House
of Livia

Temple
of Cybele

House of
Augustus

Vicus Tuscus

8 Circ
Max

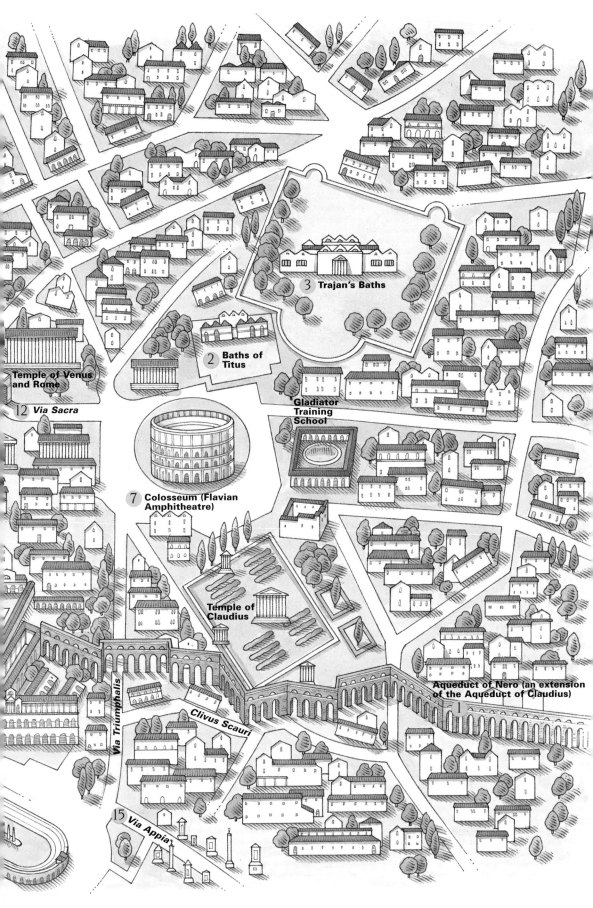

3 Trajan's Baths

2 Baths of Titus

Temple of Venus and Rome

12 *Via Sacra*

Gladiator Training School

7 Colosseum (Flavian Amphitheatre)

Temple of Claudius

Aqueduct of Nero (an extension of the Aqueduct of Claudius)

1

Via Triumphalis

Clivus Scauri

15 *Via Appia*

THE COLOSSEUM

In future centuries, the **Colosseum** stadium will be famous worldwide, but ask for it in Rome and you'll receive blank stares. It's still called the **Flavian Amphitheatre**, after the family who had it built. It won't get the name Colosseum until Hadrian has the statue of Nero, known as the Colossus, moved beside it from its present site by Trajan's Baths.

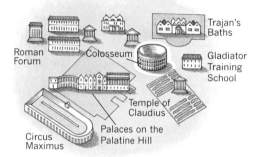

THE BUILDING

Whatever you call it, the Colosseum is a stunning arena for "the Games" – spectacular (but bloodthirsty) shows. Seating 50,000, it's divided into three:

A **The arena**: the name comes from the *harena* (sand) spread on the floor. Underneath runs a network of passages, storing scenery, cages for wild animals, and mechanisms to hoist them to the surface.

B **The podium**: a broad terrace on top of the arena wall. The best spot is reserved for the Emperor; remaining seats are taken by senators and foreign ambassadors.

C **The cavea**: this is divided into three tiers of seats separated by landings, reached by staircases and 160 passages.

GETTING IN AND OUT

There are 80 entrance arches, all numbered except for the four main entrances. Free tickets are given out early in the morning. Each ticket has a number which matches an arch. You enter through the arch with the same number as your ticket.

Only men are allowed in the first two tiers of the *cavea*. Women must sit above them, separated by a wall. Behind the women, against the outer wall, is standing room for slaves. Don't let the number of people overwhelm you. The building can be evacuated in ten minutes.

The velarium is a vast sunshade, like a sail, which is dragged across the top of the arena using ropes and pulleys.

The entrance between arches 38 and 39 is reserved for the Emperor.

THE SHOW

If you're determined to risk a visit, it's not all bad, though the bad is horrific. Usually, the performance opens with a procession and pantomime show. This often includes conjurors, though you'll probably be too high up to appreciate them. There are also circus acts – panthers pulling chariots and elephants tracing Latin phrases in the sand with their trunks. But if this sounds too much like animal cruelty to you, don't hang around.

The high wall around the arena is to protect the audience from the animals.

B

The Imperial box

The Colosseum has a circumference of 527m (1,730ft) and is 57m (187ft) tall. The arena measures 76 x 46m (249 x 151ft).

The building is made of a white stone called travertine, brought in from quarries outside Rome.

GLADIATORS

The Colosseum is known for its battles to the death between men, women and animals. Victims are criminals and prisoners of war, but Rome also has hundreds of fighting professionals called gladiators. Many are slaves given the chance to go to training school where they learn to fight. A few become rich and famous; most die young. Below are five types:

Samnite: heavily armed with sword, shield and helmet with visor

Murmillo: also heavily armed; wears a helmet crowned with a fish

Thracian: curved dagger and small, round, bronze shield

Secutor – "pursuer": fights with sword; wears helmet, shield and protection on his sword arm

Retiarius – "net fighter": fights with a net and trident; has one arm protected

WARNING!

The shows – wholesale slaughter in the name of entertainment – are not for the squeamish. You may prefer to admire the building from the outside alone. Rome is more than guts and gore, though you could be forgiven for forgetting it at the Colosseum.

143

CHARIOT RACING

If you want to rest your feet (though not your lungs), see a sporting event and spend a day at the races. Chariot racing is one of the most popular spectator sports in Rome. It's certainly less violent than the Games, though it is dangerous and accidents are common.

GOING TO THE RACES

Races take place at "circuses": purpose-built buildings which house the racetracks. There are five or six in Rome, but the oldest and most famous is the **Circus Maximus**. It's the largest in the empire, seating up to 250,000 people. The stadium starts filling up at dawn, so set out early or hire someone to save you a seat. As there's no entry fee, it's worth it. Men should wear togas: the races are only for citizens and their families.

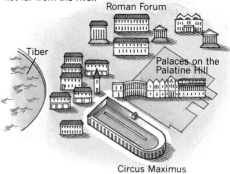

The Circus Maximus stands in front of the palaces on the Palatine Hill not far from the river.

Roman Forum

Tiber

Palaces on the Palatine Hill

Circus Maximus

At the entrance, there are three arcades decorated with marble. Here you'll find wine sellers and pastry cooks. It's a good idea to stock up on refreshments before you go in, or you'll spend the day fighting your way through crowds rather than watching the races.

An overhead view of the Circus Maximus.

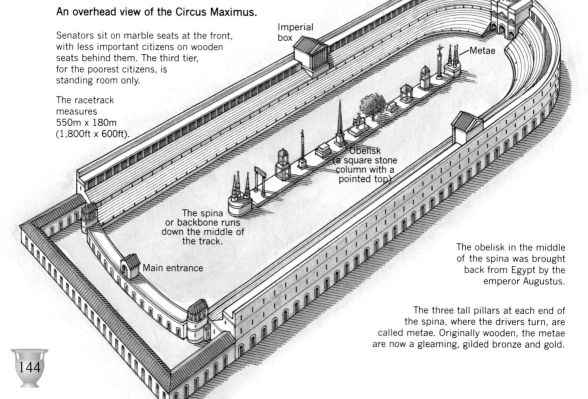

Senators sit on marble seats at the front, with less important citizens on wooden seats behind them. The third tier, for the poorest citizens, is standing room only.

The racetrack measures 550m x 180m (1,800ft x 600ft).

Imperial box

Metae

Obelisk (a square stone column with a pointed top)

The spina or backbone runs down the middle of the track.

Main entrance

The obelisk in the middle of the spina was brought back from Egypt by the emperor Augustus.

The three tall pillars at each end of the spina, where the drivers turn, are called metae. Originally wooden, the metae are now a gleaming, gilded bronze and gold.

TOP TIPS FOR TOURISTS
No. 11: Fanatical fans

Whatever happens, DON'T get carried away with excitement and cheer your team, "Come on you Reds!" if you're in a crowd of another team's supporters. Fans support their teams with a passion and it won't go down well. Remember: some Romans look upon a violent brawl as just another part of a fun day out.

BEFORE THE RACE

Like many events here, the spectacle begins with a procession. First, a band leads on the dignitary, often a consul, who is to start the races. He's accompanied by his attendants, who are followed by singers, and priests carrying images of the gods. All this happens to tremendous applause.

The excitement reaches fever pitch if the Emperor attends to start the races and takes his place in the box overlooking the finishing line. You'll feel the tension mount as the white cloth, which signals the start of each race, is raised and dropped. The twelve gates at the start line open and the drivers charge out on their chariots, going counterclockwise around the track.

"...AND THEY'RE OFF!"

Each race – and there are 24 a day – lasts seven laps and covers about eight kms (six miles). There can be up to 12 drivers in a race, racing for one of four teams: the Blues, the Reds, the Greens or the Whites. You'll see races for two, three or four-horse chariots. The more horses, the harder the chariot is to control.

As each lap is completed, a marker in the form of a golden egg or dolphin is turned on a rack on the spina.

Things get dangerous as drivers jostle for position, when rounding the bend at each end of the track. If a driver falls, it's onto sand, but he has to be quick to leap out of the way of the other chariots thundering past. The race winner receives a palm leaf of victory, a purse of gold and instant fame. Even horses can become celebrities in their own right.

Drivers wrap the reins around their waists. Each driver carries a knife to cut himself free if his chariot overturns.

SEEING A PLAY

A less grisly outing than the Games, though not always by much, is a trip to see a play. Even if you're not that interested in Roman drama, it's worth a visit for the buildings alone.

A curtain is raised in front of the stage for scenery changes.

This stage is made of stone, unlike the earliest versions, which were wooden and temporary.

Changing rooms for the actors are on either side of the stage.

Seats are allocated according to status: the rich (as ever) at the front.

❝ If you're going to a play, take plenty of cushions. The stone seats are uncomfortable to sit on for more than half an hour. ❞

A numb-bottomed drama fan

The Theatrum Pompeii (built for Pompey), which holds 27,000 people, was the first to be built of stone, in 55BC. Handier for the sightseer, though, is the Theatrum Marcelli (built for Marcellus), which stands alongside the Circus Maximus.

TOP TIPS FOR TOURISTS
No. 12: 'Tis the season

Choose the dates of your visit carefully if you want to see a play. They're only performed between April and November, and then only on certain days.

AUDIENCE REACTION

At home, you may be used to watching plays in respectful silence. Not so here. The audience gets very involved, screaming, booing and hissing as the play progresses. It's not uncommon for riots to break out in the middle of a performance, as people debate the merits of the different actors.

PLAY OR PANTOMIME?

Don't be misled by the grand buildings. Plays don't always live up to the elegance of their surroundings. This is partly because of size: the **Theatrum Marcelli** (built for Marcellus), seats 14,000. Such a vast, open-air performance area is not the place for subtlety.

In fact, recent years have seen a dramatic change in the style of plays. Large crowds, remote from the action on stage, cannot follow complicated plots. So, speeches have been cut and plays reduced to a chorus singing songs, with actors miming the action. Bawdy comedies are the most popular, though a new and brutal realism sometimes creeps in, as actors try to outdo the Games for blood and gore.

Masks are painted to look natural, but in bold shades to stand out.

STEREOTYPES

To make plays simple and easily understood, characters are reduced to stereotypes, such as "wise old man" or "smiling fool". The actors' faces can't be seen from high up, so they wear masks with strong expressions. Masks are often dark or pale, to indicate whether the character is male or female. Behind the masks, though, all actors are male.

MIME

Mime is becoming increasingly popular and, here, none of the usual conventions apply. The actors wear normal clothes, there are no masks – and even women are allowed to take part. The emphasis is still on realism, though. You may find some shows too realistic for comfort.

KEY TO COSTUMES

Actors' robes are designed to show who they are playing:

Red robes signify a poor person.

Slave characters wear plain tunics.

Purple robes indicate a rich citizen.

The costumes of elderly characters tend to be white.

Actors portraying young characters will wear several shades.

ARCHITECTURAL ART

Roman architecture, decoratively at least, borrows heavily from the Greeks. But the Romans' real interest in architecture is a far more practical one. They need massive aqueducts to carry vast supplies of water, and large arenas to cope with an ever-expanding viewing public. It is these requirements, combined with innovations in engineering, which have resulted in some spectacular pieces of architecture.

SPOTTER'S GUIDE TO COLUMNS

Columns are everywhere in Greek and therefore Roman architecture. If you like looking out for things while you're sightseeing, keep this page open and see how many of each column you can spot. Three – the Corinthian, Ionic and Doric – are based on Greek designs. The Composite is a combination of the Corinthian and Ionic columns, while only the Tuscan is all Roman.

The five columns used in Roman buildings are shown below. At one end of the scale, Corinthian columns are used for temples and palaces.

ARCHES

Arches were introduced by the Etruscans, but the Romans have developed their use into a fine art. Before the Romans, most buildings were topped off with beams of wood or stone. The invention of the arch means builders can now span much greater distances.

VAULTS

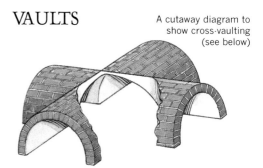

A cutaway diagram to show cross-vaulting (see below)

Often dismissed as architectural copycats, the Romans have some great inventions to their name, including tunnel vaults – arches placed side by side to form a tunnel. From tunnel vaults came cross-vaulting: two tunnel vaults meeting at right angles to each other.

DOMES

But perhaps most spectacular of all is another invention created from arches: the dome. This is made by crossing lots of arches over each other, to enclose a circular area.

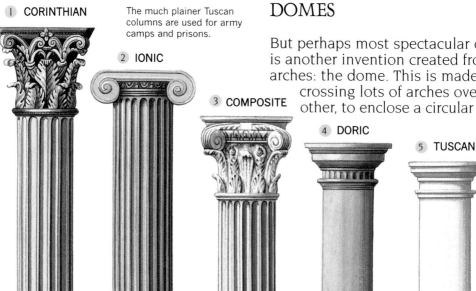

① CORINTHIAN

The much plainer Tuscan columns are used for army camps and prisons.

② IONIC

③ COMPOSITE

④ DORIC

⑤ TUSCAN

THE PANTHEON

The **Pantheon**, currently being rebuilt under Hadrian, is planned to have the largest dome in existence. Also known as the "Temple to all the gods", it will be the city's most stunning monument when finished.

The opening will measure a vast 8.8m (30ft) across, a daring feat of engineering.

Like most Roman temples, the original Pantheon was based on a Greek design. Hadrian's will retain the same style for the *portico*, or porch. Past the entrance, though, all similarity to Greek temples will end.

The outer walls will be 6m (20ft) thick. Roman engineers don't know how to reinforce concrete with metal.

An artist's impression of how the Pantheon will look when finished

Inside and out, the roof will be covered with sheets of bronze.

The squares in the roof are coffers, shaped by blocks of wood which will support the dome until the concrete sets.

Heavy concrete will be used at the base of the dome, then lighter materials higher up.

Seven alcoves are to be set in the walls, each to hold a giant statue of a god.

From the outside, the Pantheon will be impressive enough. But inside, the hall's sheer size and the magical quality of the light will take your breath away. An *oculus* (circular opening) in the roof will let sunlight stream through (not to mention rain if it's wet). Visitors who stay a while, will see the light move around the dome as the earth turns.

TOP TIPS FOR TOURISTS
No. 13: A building site

To see the construction in progress, pop along to the site. There are no barriers to keep you out but take care – there won't be any hard hats on offer.

MILITARY PROCESSIONS

All roads may lead to Rome, but inside the city, the most famous is the **Via Sacra** (Sacred Way). Pick a spot along it to see military processions, as they pass by on their way to the **Capitoline Hill**, to give thanks for victory. Such displays not only celebrate success in battle, they're the perfect way to emphasize the power and grandeur of Rome.

A military procession will surely be one of the most stirring sights you'll encounter during your visit.

A wreath of laurel leaves, worn by emperors instead of a crown

A standard

The General

A soldier called the Aquilifer walks near the head of the procession, wearing a lion skin. He carries the standard of his century*, topped with an eagle.

MARCHING ORDERS

At the head of the procession are the magistrates and senators, the leaders of Rome. They're followed by the spoils of war – the treasures and prisoners taken from the defeated enemy, sometimes carried on litters for the crowd to see.

Then come the soldiers, their uniforms gleaming, and wagons with people enacting key episodes from the campaign. Look out for the General and, more particularly, the slave standing behind him in the chariot.

The slave will be holding a wreath over the General's head. As the General acknowledges the cheers of the crowd, the slave is constantly whispering in his ear, "Remember you are but mortal." (He wouldn't say that to the Emperor!)

Each legion* has its own standard. With every successful campaign, another symbol is added to it.

*A century is a group of 80 soldiers; a legion is made up of around 5,000 men: see pages 172-173.

150

TRIUMPHAL ARCHES

Arches have sprung up all over Rome, as successive emperors commemorate their victories. Of these, the carvings on **Trajan's Arch**, which stands on the **Via Appia**, are especially worth seeing.

Standing beside a colossal arch, you'll begin to appreciate the Romans' skills as engineers.

TITUS

The **Arch of Titus**, situated close to the **Temple of Venus and Rome**, spans the *Via Sacra* as it runs between the Colosseum and the Forum. It was built to celebrate Titus' victory at the fall of Jerusalem in AD70 – the culmination of a campaign his father Vespasian had waged for the previous four years. The arch is built entirely of marble and was only completed after Titus' early death.

On the arch are some of the most spectacular sculptures of any arch in Rome, including Titus triumphant in his chariot, and a procession displaying the treasures pillaged from the temple in Jerusalem.

Below is a detail from the Arch of Titus, showing a victorious procession with captured loot. This detail is found on the inside of the arch.

TOP TIPS FOR TOURISTS
No. 14: Watch your language

If your Latin is up to it, in among the cheers you may hear the odd insult being hurled at the generals. It's considered good luck, but *only* when shouted by soldiers. Don't try it yourself or your luck will swiftly change...

DOLABELLA

The **Arch of Dolabella**, which stands at the end of the *Via Claudia*, carries **Nero's Aqueduct** which supplies water to the Palatine Hill.

AUGUSTUS

Between the temples of **Castor** and **Caesar** in the Roman Forum, look for the **Arch of Augustus**, built to celebrate Augustus' victory over Mark Antony, a Roman consul, and Cleopatra, the Queen of Egypt.

TOMBS AND CATACOMBS

Aside from military processions, you'll probably see at least one important funeral procession during your stay too. The mortality rate is high, especially for children, and few people live beyond 50.

Funerals are a chance for a family to show off its wealth and status. As such, they can be very elaborate. Don't be surprised to see the body itself. It's carried on an open litter, sometimes posed sitting up, so that everyone can see who has died.

First, the body is washed and covered in oil. If the person was a senator, he is dressed in his official robes. Then the body is covered in flowers and wreaths, before lying on display for several days, for visitors to pay their last respects.

On the day of the funeral, the procession heads first to the forum where a speech is made praising the person, before he is buried outside the city. With space at a premium inside, the law requires that all graves are outside the city walls.

Trumpeters lead the rest of the procession if the funeral is for an adult.

Actors wearing realistic masks, complete with hair, represent the dead person's famous ancestors.

Dozens of musicians and professional mourners join family and friends, accompanying the body on its final journey.

Black animals are also included in the procession – for sacrifice.

FUNERAL CUSTOMS AND BELIEFS

The dead person is dressed in his finest clothes, with a coin placed under his tongue. Like the Greeks*, the Romans believe that after death a person is ferried to the underworld (Hades), across the river Styx. The coin is to pay the ferryman.

It's put into the person's mouth as their hands are often filled with cakes to feed Cerberus, the three-headed dog who guards Hades. On arrival in the underworld, a person's spirit is judged and sent either to *Elysium* (heaven) or *Tartarus* (hell).

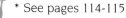

* See pages 114-115

COLOSSEUM

THE APPIAN WAY

Many tombs lie along the **Appian Way**, or *Via Appia*, the main road leading out of Rome to the south.

A journey along the Appian Way makes for an interesting excursion. Most of the tombs are grand affairs and you can learn a great deal about Roman life from reading people's histories on their tombs.

You can pick up a litter or a carriage from the stables at one of the gates leading out of the city. There's no system of inspections though, and not all stables are reputable, so check your horse before you ride.

Tombs often have elaborate carvings which show an aspect of the dead person's life.

The Appian Way is 122 miles (196 kms) long and sees a constant stream of traffic.

CATACOMBS

Traditionally, funerals ended with a cremation, though burials have recently come into fashion. For a more gruesome trip, visit a catacomb or *columbarium* – which store dead bodies or urns full of ashes respectively. But be careful: the chambers are used by outlawed groups, such as Christians, for secret meetings. If you come across such a group, leave quickly or you risk arrest.

TOP TIPS FOR TOURISTS
No. 15: Crocodile tears

The Romans hire professional mourners, called *praeficae*, to grieve at their funerals. It's a job you might consider if your money runs out. You'll be given a tear bottle in which to catch your tears. But don't spill any – mourners are paid by the amount they shed. To make sure the tears flow, you might find it helps to go via a market to pick up a raw onion.

A tear bottle

OSTIA

153

DAY-TO-DAY SHOPPING

Whether you're looking for souvenirs of your stay or something for supper, Rome has shops and markets to suit every taste, not to mention each purse. The more exclusive shops, and markets for fresh produce, are found in the fora (see pages 158-159), but the shops for everyday goods are housed on the ground floors of buildings.

Most have a counter across the front, over which you choose and buy the goods. You'll find everything from bacon to pots and pans, oil lamps and cloth. Not everyone can afford the luxury of a shop. Many people offer their goods or services from portable stalls set up by the road.

The portable stall of a cutler (someone who makes and sharpens knives)

CRAFTSMEN AT WORK

Virtually everything that has to be manufactured – bread from flour, for example, or tables and chairs from timber – is made on the premises. So, even if there's nothing you need, you can enjoy the spectacle of goods being produced right in front of you.

Craftsmen in the shops along the street might not sell goods of the quality of those found in a forum, but they're equally fascinating to watch. Even making the most mundane cookware requires a skilled potter, and you can easily spend half an hour watching one throw dishes and plates on his wheel.

A view of a street from the back of shops. The shoppers are mostly slaves, for whom shopping is a daily chore.

Metalworkers making household tools

TOP TIPS FOR TOURISTS
No. 16: Eco-packaging

Rome is a truly eco-friendly city when it comes to packaging – shopkeepers just don't use any. Everything is sold unwrapped, so bring a basket from home or buy one before you shop. For oil or wine, you'll need to bring your own bottles or jugs.

Oil lamps are the only form of artificial light apart from candles.

FAST FOOD

Peer into the back of any bakery you pass and you'll see slaves turning a large stone mill, to grind flour. With bread baking in stone ovens as you watch – and smell – you'll find it hard to resist.

If you'd like to drizzle olive oil on your hot-from-the-oven purchase, visit one of the numerous olive oil shops. Many have their own presses to squeeze the oil from the fruit. The oil is stored in large jars called *amphorae* which are lowered into the ground to keep cool.

NEW SHOES

Having pounded the streets sightseeing, you may need a new pair of sandals. These too are made on the spot. Visit a shoemaker, who will make a pair to your measurements.

A pair of hand made sandals

OPENING HOURS

With poor artificial light, Romans make the most of daylight hours. Since all deliveries must be made before dawn anyway, shops open early. They close at noon for the hottest part of the day, when you'd be advised to follow the Roman lead and have a siesta. Shops reopen in the afternoon and shut at dusk.

Aching feet? Visit a pharmacist. They have a wide selection of herbal ointments and potions, including those to soothe the sole! And if they fail, you can always ask for a magic spell. But be warned. They're not cheap and I've never found one which worked.

A footsore shopper

An oil shop – oil is used for cooking, washing and lighting.

An amphora

In this bakery, slaves are working the mill but it's not unusual to see a donkey turning it.

An olive press

155

A SHOPPER'S PARADISE

For the ritzier and most exclusive boutiques, head upmarket to one of the fora. As a rule of thumb, the closer you get to any forum, the more fashionable the shops become, selling more exotic items (in Roman eyes at least), such as books and fine cloth. Prices are expensive but generally not outrageous. If you can't afford them, you can at least enjoy browsing with senators and their wives.

SPECIALIST STREETS

Of all the streets in Rome the **Vicus Tuscus** is probably the best-known for shopping. It's named after the Etruscan merchants who own most of the shops. Here, you'll find the finest silks, imported from the Greek island of Kos. Close by are specialist perfumiers, who will make you up a scent from your choice of fragrances, not to mention shops selling cosmetics and highly decorated and polished, silver mirrors.

A perfume bottle

THE ORIGINAL KEYRING

One very useful souvenir is a lockable casket for valuables. It comes with a key designed to be worn as a ring.

Keyrings are made of iron, rather than silver or gold which would be too soft.

GLASSWARE

One item you may wish to buy in the forum – it's a little cheaper than gold or silver – is glassware. Glass has become fashionable in wealthy households, as you'll see from the quality and choice on offer. (Poorer households make do with pottery cups and jugs.) Available glass varies from the almost (but not entirely) transparent to opaque.

Glassblowers heat the glass in ovens shaped like beehives.

COLLECTABLES

With the Romans' admiration for Greek art, there's a current craze for all things Greek. You can't move for the antique Greek vases and statues everywhere. All of Rome is collecting them, from the Emperor down, so you're bound to find something in your price range. If you're on a spending spree, you could consider an Etruscan bronze or a citrus wood table. They're very expensive, though, and less transportable than a vase.

Be careful! That statue impulse buy could prove difficult to take home.

JEWELS AND BANGLES

Along the south side of the **Basilica Aemilia**, in the **Roman Forum**, are shops belonging to the gold and silversmiths. They make exquisite bracelets, brooches, necklaces, rings and tiaras, all with fantastic designs. You'll notice well-off Roman women go overboard, positively draping themselves in the stuff.

A necklace of solid gold and a cameo brooch. The bracelet, of a snake, is worn on the upper arm.

> ❝ *If you can afford a gold bracelet, ask for it to be engraved with a good luck message. But if you want it in any language other than Latin, you'll have to write it down.* ❞
>
> *A poor but happy visitor*

"BOOKS"

For books or, rather, scrolls head to the **Argiletum**, which runs alongside the Basilica Aemilia. Watching 20 or so slaves laboriously copying out scrolls for sale, you'll realize why they are are so rare and expensive. Since they also rely on the accuracy of the copyists, no two copies of one scroll are the same.

Scrolls are made of sheets of papyrus stuck together (see page 171).

People are hired to read manuscripts aloud to scribes, who each take down a copy.

COSMETICS

Wealthy Roman women have a personal make-up artist, an *ornatrix*, to make them up each day. Even if you can't afford that, you might like to buy some Roman cosmetics. There's a wide selection, all made from natural, if strange, ingredients, such as wood ash and red wine.

TOP TIPS FOR TOURISTS
No. 17: Caveat emptor

When shopping, bear in mind the Roman phrase (still used in the 21st century): *Caveat emptor!* ("Buyer Beware!") and check goods carefully before you pay for them.

MARKETS

At the other end of the scale from the exclusive shops in the forum are the market stalls. The markets are set up in the central areas of *fora* and found all over the city.

Some specialize in just one product and these generally open one day a week. Others are open daily, and sell a whole variety of things. You'll find cabbages and beans alongside stalls selling woollen cloth or earthenware jugs.

TRAJAN'S MARKET

The markets in the **Imperial Fora** are close together, a bonus if you like to compare prices of goods before buying (see the plan on page 140). But if you only go to one, make it **Trajan's Market**, overlooking his forum. Despite its name, this is no mere collection of stalls, but 150 shops and offices on terraces. Fruit and flowers are sold on the lower levels, with oil, vinegar and imported items higher up. Don't miss the fifth floor, with its fantastic view, and fishponds where you can buy fish so fresh they're still swimming.

Trajan's Market

The shops and offices are ranged on terraces over five floors.

Offices on the upper levels are used to hand out free corn to Rome's unemployed.

Shops on the ground floor are smaller and cooler than those above.

TOP TIPS FOR TOURISTS
No. 18: An early start

If you want the freshest produce, try to be at the market as it opens – your fellow shoppers, mostly slaves, will be up well before dawn.

FARM FRESH

A huge variety of produce is brought in daily from farms outside the city. Don't expect to buy potatoes, peppers or tomatoes though – or chocolate. They come from Central America which has no trading links with Rome. In fact, the Romans don't even know the American continent exists.

Market stall traders only sell organic produce, as Roman farmers don't use pesticides. (They have no choice – pesticides haven't been invented yet.)

A slave auction taking place: slaves wear signs around their necks advertising their skills. Most are prisoners of war.

A FAIR DEAL

To ensure you aren't cheated, government officials called *aediles* make regular visits to the markets, checking both the quality of goods on sale and testing the weights and measures for accuracy.

Your goods will either be weighed on a simple balance, or a device called a steelyard. Various amounts are marked off along the bar. The stallholder moves the weight along it, until the scale balances.

A steelyard

Weights can be intricately carved, often portraying the heads of famous emperors and generals.

SLAVE AUCTION

One of the most commonly traded commodities, after food and wine, is people. This will prove something of a culture shock to many visitors. Though it is offensive to tourists from later times, Romans accept the practice without question.

Slaves are bought like any other property and sold off to the highest bidder. Their subsequent treatment depends wholly on the kindness or otherwise of their master. Not all slaves become menial servants however. Many, in particular those from Greece, find work as doctors, tutors or librarians.

> **❝***The flower stalls are amazing, with hundreds of brilliant blooms. You can't miss them: they're next to the fish stalls, in an attempt to hide the smell. Buy huge bunches of the cheapest flowers, to freshen up a stuffy apartment.* **❞**
>
> *A tourist who missed air freshener*

THE PORT OF ROME

If you want to see where all the goods you've bought enter the city, visit the **Port of Rome** just downstream from the **Theatrum Marcelli**. You can easily spend a pleasant hour or two, watching barges being pulled up the **Tiber**.

The Port of Rome

The barges set out from the sea port of **Ostia**, some 25kms (15 miles) outside the city. Cargoes from merchant ships are unloaded onto barges at Ostia, for the final leg of the journey to Rome. Barges moor by the **Pons Aemilius**, which dates back to the second century BC and was the first bridge to span the river.

ON THE WHARF

Along the banks of the Tiber, you'll see the gigantic warehouses, or *horrea*, where the barges are unloaded. Some specialize in only one product, such as pepper or spices. You can tell the latter by the fragrant smells which linger in the air. Others are general stores, hoarding wine, oil, marble, cloth, timber, wool, tiles – the list is almost endless. Keep an eye out for flying pottery as you walk around. Jars which have contained olive oil can't be reused, so they're smashed on the quay and used as ballast to weigh down ships.

Olive oil jars being shattered at the dockside.

A Roman carving of a laden barge, part of a merchant's tomb.

160

WHOLESALE MARKETS

To see where shopkeepers buy their
supplies, and gain an insight into
the sheer scale of Roman trade,
visit the Forum Holitorium and the
Forum Boarium. They're right next
to the Port of Rome.

The **Forum Holitorium**, which sells
fruit and vegetables, lies at the foot
of the Capitoline Hill.

The **Forum Boarium** is the cattle
and poultry market. It's situated
beside the Annona, facing the Tiber,
with temples in among the livestock.

There are round temples to
Hercules and Portunus, the
god of rivers and ports,
in the cattle market.

THE ANNONA

The **Annona** is the massive state
warehouse where free corn for
Rome's unemployed is stored and
distributed. At least a third of
Rome's population depends on this
"corn dole" for survival. Men line up
for a wooden tablet to prove their
family's entitlement. But three
groups of people are ineligible:
soldiers, slaves, and visitors
passing through the city, so don't
be tempted to join the line.

Goods stored in warehouses
are sold to traders and
the general
public.

HERCULES AND THE COWS

*Legend says that Hercules drove
cattle through the Forum Boarium.
He rested by the Tiber where Cacus,
a three-headed, fire-breathing
monster, tried to steal some cows.
Cacus hoped to avoid detection by
making them walk facing the wrong
way. But Hercules saw through the
trick and slew him on the spot.*

OSTIA

Ostia is well worth a couple of days' visit if you're thinking of venturing out of the city. The main seaport of Rome, it stands at the mouth of the Tiber. It's a bustling place, with slaves unloading cargoes, and scribes busily recording every last *amphora* of olive oil.

The three ports of Ostia

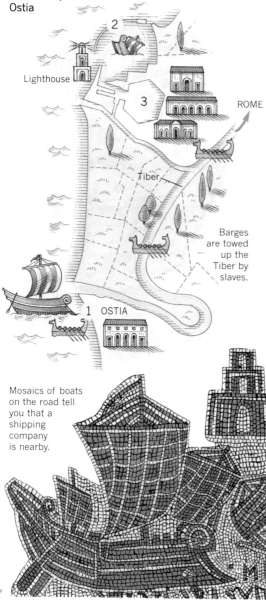

Lighthouse

2

3

ROME

1 OSTIA

Tiber

Barges are towed up the Tiber by slaves.

Mosaics of boats on the road tell you that a shipping company is nearby.

Government officials are on hand to direct operations and merchants, or their stewards, hover nearby, keeping an eagle eye on their investments.

THREE PORTS IN ONE

As it's 25 times cheaper to send goods by sea than land, the port sees huge business. With hundreds of ships coming and going, the original port 1 couldn't cope, so two more were built: one begun by Claudius in AD42, the most recent by Trajan in AD103. But Claudius' port 2 was open to the weather and in AD62, 200 ships sank, after taking shelter from a storm. Trajan's port 3 – shaped like a hexagon – can safely moor more than 300 ships at a time.

ART AT YOUR FEET

One of the most popular art forms in Rome is mosaics: pictures made from tiny tiles. Ostia has a fine example of mosaic art right under your feet. Look for it in the **Square of Corporations** near the playhouse. The Square houses the various businesses which operate from the port. Mosaics on the street outside their offices advertise their trades.

Cargoes unloaded straight onto barges are carried up the Tiber to Rome.

Other goods are unloaded onto the quay to be stored in warehouses.

FOOD CHAIN

Food is an essential import for a city of over a million people. The market farms around Rome can never hope to produce enough, so food, mainly grain, is brought in from other parts of the empire. Grain from Africa, Egypt and Syria, weighing more than 40,000 elephants, passes through Ostia each year on its way to Rome.

66 All that trade and ships may bring reaches Rome ... ... So many cargoes arrive, that the city seems like a common warehouse of the world. 99

Aelius Aristides

IMPORTS

Grain forms just a tiny part of Rome's vast import trade, with huge quantities of goods arriving every day. Spain alone supplies a variety of food – olive oil, fruit, honey and salt fish – as well as wax, wool and cloth, silver, lead and red dye. Marble and purple dye come from Greece, papyrus (for books) from Egypt, spices and gems from India, silks from the Far East, glass from Syria, and amber from the Baltic.

BOAT-SPOTTING

The largest cargo ships can be up to 30m (100ft) long and 9m (30ft) wide, and are designed to hold immense cargoes. A ship might be carrying 6,000 *amphorae* full of wine, a weighty load of timber, or giraffes for the Games. Reliant on the wind to power their huge sails, ships can reach a top speed of only 7km an hour (just over 4 miles an hour). No wonder it can take up to three weeks to get from North Africa to Rome.

163

A WEEK IN THE COUNTRY

If the heat of the city gets to you, and you feel like a change, do as the Romans do and head to the country. You may meet someone who invites you to stay, or even offers to lend you their *villa* (country house) for a week or two.

After the city crowds and grime, you'll think you are in another world. Villas can be magnificent affairs: spacious houses, set in landscaped gardens, with pools, fountains and statues.

LIFE ON THE FARM

City people idealize country life and certainly, as the guest of a wealthy villa owner, you'll have a restful break. Such villas are actually lavish farmhouses, however. For the slaves who work on them, the harsh reality is long hours of backbreaking toil.

Most villas have an orchard to provide fresh fruit such as plums and figs.

Estates contain everything the family needs to be self-sufficient: living quarters, stabling, rooms to store crops – even a bakery and bathhouse.

Stabling for animals is at the back of the villa.

In front of the villa and within its walls, are formal gardens. The fields for crops are some distance from the house.

Inside, villas are richly decorated. This "window" is part of a wall painting.

FARM PRODUCE

Cereals, grapes for wine, and olives for oil are the crops most often grown for sale by Roman farmers. They grow fruit and vegetables too, but these are for the dozens of people living and working on the estate. Fruit and vegetables for commercial use are produced by the numerous market gardeners on the outskirts of Rome. Ducks, chickens and geese are also raised, solely to supply the estate's needs.

COUNTRY FOOD

Country estates often have a pond to provide fresh fish for the dinner table, and the surrounding countryside offers a ready supply of game, including deer, boar and pheasant. Oxen are kept too, both for working in the wheat fields and for their leather hides.

WINE BUFFS

If grapes are the main crop at the estate where you're staying, you may get to see them harvested and processed – though watching wine-making may put you off the finished product. Once the grapes have been picked, they are poured into a stone vat and trampled on by barefooted slaves, to extract as much juice as possible. The last drops are then squeezed out with a press, before the liquid is stored in jars to ferment.

Slaves stuck with this sticky task hold onto poles to keep themselves from slipping.

The liquid either goes straight into jars or, when produced on a larger scale, is piped into another vat first.

TOP TIPS FOR TOURISTS
No. 20: Getting there

If you don't have a friend who will lend you their carriage for a week, you can rent a wagon at the city gates. You will need to allow several days for your journey, but there are various state-run guesthouses along the way, for overnight stops.

HEALTH SPAS

Many villas have bathhouses attached, but for an extra lift, you could visit a mineral bath, offering smelly but revitalizing treatments.

BESIDE THE SEASIDE

If your villa is anywhere near the coast, it's worth extending your vacation to go to the seaside. The resorts of Capri and Naples are particularly popular, and their villas are often the last word in luxury. The beaches are clean, the sea inviting and, in Capri, there are regular boat trips for visitors around the bay.

66 *Why tire yourself in Rome, always bowing down to wealthy patrons*, *when you can be rich with the spoils of the woods and fields?* 99
Martial

*Patrons are wealthy Romans who offer financial help and protection to poorer citizens, or those without families, in return for their political support.

RELIGION AND FESTIVALS

All life in Rome is closely connected with religion. There's a god or goddess (or minor spirit) for almost any activity you can think of. Religion itself is very much divided between public (or state) and private.

STATE RELIGION

State religion, run by paid priests and priestesses, is based around rituals performed at elaborate ceremonies. These are held in the sacred spaces in front of temples. People only enter temples if they have a special request. Inside, temples house treasure, gifts from worshippers and statues.

Ceremonies take place outside the temple, where there is room for crowds.

State worship focuses on *Roma*, goddess of Rome, other state deities (see right), and deified dead emperors. The state even tolerates foreign deities: the Romans are so anxious not to offend any gods in existence, they often take on those of their defeated enemies.

GODS & GODDESSES

Listed below are some of the most important state deities:-

Jupiter: King of the gods

Juno: Jupiter's wife, the goddess of women and marriage

Juno, often shown with a peacock

Minerva: Goddess of war and wisdom

A statue of Jupiter

Mars: God of war

Venus: Goddess of love and beauty

Mercury: God of trade and thieves, and Jupiter's messenger

Vesta: Goddess of the hearth

Mercury, with his winged sandals and voyager's clothes

EASTERN CULTS

As the empire grows, so has the popularity of cults from abroad, such as that of Isis, a goddess from Egypt. Christianity is increasingly popular, but is fiercely opposed by the state because Christians believe in only one god. Avoid all contact with Christians if you value your life.

PRIVATE RELIGION

Religion in the home is based around prayers. Each household has its own spirits, or *Lares*, to protect them and a shrine, the *Lararium*, where the family prays and offers small gifts of fruit and wine. Each family also has a *genius* (guardian spirit) and *manes* (ancestral spirits) to watch over them. There are even spirits of the pantry, called *penates*.

TELLING THE FUTURE

The Romans are great believers in supernatural forces, consulting all kinds of experts to tell them what the gods think of their plans. You could try it – but don't take it too seriously.

Haruspex: a priest who examines the innards of sacrificed animals to look for signs of disease. A damaged liver might show that the gods disapprove of a project.

A bronze plaque of a haruspex

Augurs: 16 prophets who look for ominous signs in nature, by studying things such as cloud shapes, flocks of birds or lightning.

Sibyl: a prophetess who wrote books during the early Republic, with advice on interpreting the will of the gods.

Astrologers: tell a person's fortune, by studying the position of the stars at the time of his birth.

CALENDAR OF FESTIVALS

There are over 200 festivals, only a few of which can be listed, so your trip is bound to coincide with one.

FEB **Lupercalia**
15 *At a cave on the Palatine, two teams put on goatskins and race around the hill.*

MAR **Anna Perenna**
15 *Take a picnic to the Tiber – with plenty to drink. Romans believe the more they drink on this day, the longer they'll live.*

APR **Parilia**
21 *Traditionally, the day of Rome's birth. Each area of the city organizes a celebration, including bonfires and large outdoor feasts.*

APR **Ludi Florales**
28 *A carnival for Flora, goddess of flowers (one to avoid if you get hay fever). Everyone dances in floral garlands.*

JUN **Vestalia**
9 *A festival for Vesta. Note: the bakeries will be shut. The Vestal Virgins bake a special bread for the day, so bakers take the day off.*

AUG **Feast of Mercury**
12 *A massive – and free – public feast. It's funded from the 10% businessmen pay to Mercury's shrine from their profits each year.*

SEP **Ludi Romani**
5-19 *A festival of games, races and plays. If you're invited to the banquet at the Senate, don't be surprised if some guests are rather quiet. Statues of gods are dressed up and put on couches to join in.*

167

FASHION

STYLE

Most clothes for men and women are based around simple shapes and usually made from a large, rectangular piece of cloth. This is folded to be worn and held in place with a brooch called a *fibula*, or tied with a belt and buckle. As all sewing is done by hand, the Romans do as little as possible.

FABRIC

Clothes are generally made of wool or linen. Fine linen and silks are imported from Egypt and Greece, but they're extremely expensive and worn only by the seriously wealthy. Men tend to wear clothes in their natural state of cream, or bleached white, but women wear a variety of shades. Vegetable and mineral dyes are used to brighten cloth. The richer you are, the brighter and more varied your clothes.

A Roman soldier's buckle

HIS. . .

Underneath it all, men wear a loincloth. This is the only underwear they bother with and it's generally kept on at night. Over the top, they wear a simple tunic. The tunic is designed to hang slightly longer at the back than the front, which ends at the knee. Outside, they also wear cloaks.

Togas are only worn by Roman citizens and their sons. They're very heavy, not to mention tricky to wear. Try carrying on a conversation while shifting yards of cloth over a shoulder.

Older men wear longer tunics. The purple stripe shows that the wearer is a senator.

Togas are always white. To brighten things up for a party, men can wear cloaks in funkier shades; they wear dark, if not black, cloaks for solemn occasions such as funerals.

Putting on a toga

This is a complicated and time-consuming business. For those occasions where you have to wear one, here's the simple way to put it on:

1. Drape over the left shoulder.

2. Bring the other end in front of you.

3. Throw it over your left shoulder.

4. Tuck a section into your belt.

...AND HERS

Women also wear simple underwear with a plain tunic on top. Over that, they wear a long dress called a *stola*. These are plain too, although wealthier women wear stolas of silk in dazzling shades including red, yellow, purple and blue. Dressier stolas, with elaborate embroidery, are worn on special occasions.

A stola

On top of the stola, many women wear a *palla*, a long, rectangular scarf. When out of the house, most women cover themselves up, either with a veil or by wearing the palla draped over their heads.

The palla is worn like a large shawl, wrapped around the body and thrown over one shoulder.

COSMETICS

Pale skin is very much in vogue, so arms and faces are whitened with powdered chalk. Ash is used to darken eyelids and eyebrows; lips and cheeks are reddened with plant dye or the sediment from red wine.

CHILDREN

Clothes for children pretty much match those for adults. The very young run around in short tunics. But, from an early age, the sons of citizens wear a mini toga, called a *toga praetexta*, and girls a stola.

HAIR

For Roman men, the term "fashion victim" has as much – and painful – relevance as for women. Though hairstyles are simple (most men sport a close crop), they face the daily torture of a visit to the barber for a shave.

Blunt iron razors, and only water on the face beforehand, mean cuts are an unavoidable hazard. If you decide to risk a visit, you might like to bear in mind this cure to stop bleeding: spiders' webs soaked in oil and vinegar.

Poorer women pull their hair back into plain buns, but the rich suffer long hours having their hair dressed – piled high upon their heads and teased into ringlets or braids. If hair isn't naturally curly, heated tongs are used.

Blonde and red hair are currently the most fashionable. Rather than resort to dye, some women simply have a wig made from the blonde or red hair of a slave.

Dozens of hairpins, which can be made of ivory, silver, or bone like this one, hold intricate hairstyles in place.

EDUCATION

SCHOOLING

In education, as in everything else, there is a sharp divide between rich and poor. Most families can't afford to educate their offspring, sending them out to work instead. Only the children of wealthy parents are educated. The richest have a private tutor. For the rest – boys and girls – the first school, or *ludus*, begins at the age of six and lasts until they're 11.

THE *LUDUS*

The ludus usually consists of one room, on the ground floor of a *domus* or behind a shop. The school day begins at dawn and continues until noon without a break, quite a strain for the youngest pupils. Classes are small with, on average, 12 pupils per class. Most schools have one class and one teacher, often a Greek ex-slave. Schools vary but each has set fees – parents pick the one they can afford.

DISCIPLINE

Teachers are strict disciplinarians and ardent supporters of corporal punishment, with beatings a regular occurrence.

A family slave called a pedagogus takes children to and from school, and keeps an eye on them while they're there.

EQUIPMENT

Young pupils scratch their first letters on pieces of broken pottery, or wax tablets, using a metal pen called a *stylus*. Older pupils write on sheets of papyrus (see right), using reed pens, and ink made from a mixture of gum and soot. Arithmetic is equally low-tech. It's taught using fingers and an abacus.

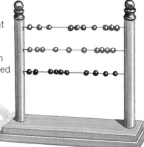

A stylus (far left) with a flat end for erasing marks on wax, a reed pen (left) and an abacus (right)

LESSONS

Lessons cover the basics: reading, writing and simple arithmetic. One of the most common teaching tools is reciting – the alphabet for the youngest children; the works of famous Greek and Roman authors for older pupils.

THE *GRAMMATICUS*

The secondary stage of education – exclusively for boys, and exclusive in every other sense – is covered by a teacher known as the *grammaticus*. He takes boys from the richest parents, from the age of 11 until at least 13 or 14. Most girls marry at 12, so they leave the ludus to learn how to run a household.

THE CURRICULUM

A carving of a boy reciting

At first sight, the curriculum taught by the grammaticus seems wide-ranging, covering history and geography, mythology, astronomy, music and mathematics. But most of the day is taken up with studying Greek *odes* (long story-telling poems), because Greek culture has such a major influence on Roman life. Many lessons consist simply of reading aloud or reciting passages which have already been learned by heart. (Dull for pupils but worse for visitors, if you were planning to visit a school.)

PUBLIC SPEAKING

Public speaking is a vital part of schooling for anyone who wants to go into law or politics. From about 13, some boys are sent to a *rhetor* to learn the art of speaking in public.

Boys are taught how to write and present speeches, using various exercises. One involves saying the same thing in a dozen different ways. The rhetor also dreams up bizarre scenarios for his pupils to debate. Training can last for years, with the luckiest being sent to Athens or Rhodes to finish their education.

CITIZEN TRAINING

The main role of the secondary stage of education, however, is to train upper class boys to take their place as Roman citizens, and prepare them for the task of ruling Rome and the empire.

MAKING "PAPER"

If you've visited Egypt, you'll have come across the reed papyrus. Like the Egyptians, the Romans use it to make paper. For those who don't know how it's made, here's a quick summary:

1 With the outer rind of the reed removed, the core is cut into strips and soaked in water.

2 Two layers of strips are pressed together at right angles. Starch in the core acts like glue.

3 The sheet is beaten with a mallet and left to dry, before being polished with a stone.

4 Lots of sheets are joined together to form a scroll. In a well-made scroll, the joins are invisible.

Pupils unrolling a scroll: since scrolls are around 10m (30ft) long, they're often fitted with wooden or ivory rollers to make them easier to handle.

THE ARMY

EMPIRE BUILDERS

It's thanks to Rome's army that the empire has reached the size and stature it has, while constant warfare with countries on all its borders has made the army an efficient and destructive fighting force.

FIGHTING FARMERS

Initially, all Roman property-owners (usually farmers) had to serve in the army. Wars were brief and near Rome, so it was almost a vacation – though a violent one to which you took your own weapons. But, soon, a more dedicated body of men was required. By 100BC, men no longer needed property to join. Soldiers were paid, and given a uniform, weapons and training.

A HARD LIFE

Life in the army is tough. Minor infringements result in flogging. Trouble-makers have their rations reduced, but in a mutinous legion, every tenth man is executed (the origin of the term "to decimate").

Route marches of 30km (18 miles) take place three times a month. Troops have to march at up to 8km (5 miles) an hour, carrying heavy packs, to prepare them for long marches on campaigns.

AN ARMY CAMP

At the end of a long day's march, soldiers have to build the overnight camp, so camps go up quickly and always in the same form:

All camps are rectangular. Inside, the tents are pitched in rows.

The General's headquarters is always in the middle of the camp.

A deep ditch is dug around the camp. A row of stakes is put in the earth thrown up from the ditch.

WEAPONS

Standard weapons issue includes: a short stabbing sword, 60cm (2ft) long, hung from the right side of the belt; a dagger, hung from the left; and two *pila* (javelins), one heavy, one light. These have wooden shafts with a middle section of soft iron, deliberately designed to bend as the spear hits its target. This is to prevent the enemy from throwing them back.

A cooking pot is just one of the many items in a soldier's pack.

A sword (gladius) in a decorated scabbard: this would belong to a general or someone of a fairly high rank.

UNIFORM

Every soldier receives a uniform, though the cost is deducted from his pay. The basic get-up is the same for all: a wool or linen tunic, with wool breeches and a cloak in colder climates. Tunics are topped with a belted shirt of fine chain mail, or a more protective leather tunic with metal strips. Everyone wears a metal helmet and carries a curved wooden and leather shield. Some soldiers also wear metal leg protectors.

Soldiers generally wear sandals, sometimes replaced with sturdy boots for marches.

ARMY DIVISIONS

Much of the army's success relies on its structured nature. 28 groups called legions, each with around 5,000 men, are divided into smaller groups, down to a group of eight men called a *contubernium*.

A contubernium: 8 men who share a tent and eat together.

10 contubernia make up 1 century of 80 men.

Centuries group together to form cohorts. Each legion is made up of 10 cohorts. The First Cohort has 10 centuries (800 men). The other nine have 6 centuries (480 men).

LEGIONS

Legions don't just contain soldiers, but doctors, clerks, priests, engineers and surveyors. They also have auxiliaries, non-citizens from the provinces, who are grouped in cohorts of 500 to 1,000 men. These earn less than legionaries and have less training. They often provide the cavalry, act as scouts and carry messages.

A senior officer called a **legate** commands each legion. Below him are six officers called **tribunes**. Each century is led by a **centurion**, who is assisted by an **optio**.

PERSONALITIES

Aquilifer: carries the legion's standard into battle, wearing a lion skin over his uniform.

Signifer: carries the century's standard; organizes the burial club for soldiers' funerals.

Praefectus castrorum: in charge of building camps; third in command after the legate and senior tribune.

Tesserarius: the army spy. Each century has a daily password, which the *tesserarius* gives the soldiers each morning.

A standard: if a legion's standard is captured, the legion is disgraced and disbanded, so a cunning enemy makes straight for the Aquilifer.

USEFUL INFORMATION

CURRENCY

During the Republic, various Roman mints each produced their own coins. Thanks to Augustus, the monetary system is standardized now and all coins have a fixed value. The most recent will show Trajan's or Hadrian's head, but coins issued under earlier emperors are still acceptable.

Aureus: gold - weighs 8g (¼ oz); the largest denomination

Denarius: silver - 25 *denarii* in an *aureus*

Sestertius: bronze - 4 *sestertii* in a *denarius*

Dupondius: bronze - 2 *dupondii* in a *sestertius*

As: copper - 4 *as* in a *sestertius*

Semi: bronze - 2 *semis* in an *as*

Quadrans: copper - 4 *quadrans* in an *as*

NUMBERS

Roman numerals are made up of a combination of the letters I, V, X, L, C, D and M. They follow a logical pattern, based on addition and subtraction. 4, for example, is written IV, meaning 1 less than 5 (V); 7 is VII, or 5 (V) plus 2 (II). But since all numbers are based around just a few letters, you are soon dealing with very long numbers. For example, it takes seven letters to write 78:

$$50 + 20 + 5 + 3 = 78$$

Numbers in Latin*:

1 **I**	11 **XI**		
2 **II**	12 **XII**	50	**L**
3 **III**	13 **XIII**		
4 **IV**	14 **XIV**	100	**C**
5 **V**	15 **XV**		
6 **VI**	16 **XVI**	200	**CC**
7 **VII**	17 **XVII**	500	**D**
8 **VIII**	18 **XVIII**		
9 **IX**	19 **XIX**	1000	**M**
10 **X**	20 **XX**		

1	*unus*	8	*octo*
2	*duo*	9	*novem*
3	*tres*	10	*decem*
4	*quattuor*	11	*undecim*
5	*quinque*	12	*duodecim*
6	*sex*	50	*quinquaginta*
7	*septem*	100	*centum*

*See page 177 for tips on how to pronounce Latin

TIME

Telling the time in Ancient Rome is a vague business. Romans rely on sundials and water clocks to tell the time,

Sundial

but neither are very accurate. Days last as long as the daylight and are divided into twelve hours.

Midday falls exactly in the middle – the point at which the sixth hour gives way to the seventh. Hours are approximate, not subdivided into minutes, and longer in the summer, when the light lasts longer.

LAUNDRY

If you have a toga, it will need specialist dry-cleaning. You can send your toga and other dirty washing to a fuller. Fullers generally treat cloth before it's made into clothes, but they also offer a cleaning service.

① First, togas are trodden in a mixture of sodium carbonate and a type of clay known as "fuller's earth".

② Then they're hung on wooden frames over chemical fires, which bleach them.

③ Finally, they're left out to dry before being folded and flattened in a giant press.

EMERGENCIES

Since 6AD, a combined police and fire-fighting force called the *Cohors Vigilum* has been in operation. They'll be on hand if your apartment catches fire, but don't expect them to do two jobs at once if your valuables are stolen.

Firemen use leather buckets and hoses.

MAIL

There's no postal service for ordinary citizens, but government mail is sent by courier. You could try charm or a bribe to have urgent letters included with the official mail. But it's really not worth it if you're only sending postcards home – they'll arrive months after you, if they arrive at all.

NEWSPAPERS

If you're fluent in Latin, a daily paper called the *Acta Diurna* – actually a single handwritten sheet – is handed out in the Forum with the latest news.

PHRASEBOOK

HANDY WORDS AND PHRASES

Hello	*salve* or *salvete**
Goodbye	*vale* or *valete**

Add *domine* (sir) for a man and *domina* (madam) for a woman.

How are you?	*vales?*
I'm well	*valeo*
I'm very well	*optime valeo*
I'm happy	*felix sum*
I'm unhappy	*tristis sum*
I'm ill	*aegroto*

Yes	*ita...* or *certe*
No	*non...* or *minime*
Thanks	*gratias ago*
Tell me	*dic*
I don't know	*nescio*
I'm sorry	*doleo*
I would like	*volo*
I don't like	*mihi non placet*
I don't want	*nolo*
I prefer	*malo*

When...?	*quando...*
Why?	*cur?*
How?	*quomodo?*
How many?	*quot?*
What time is it?	*hora quota est?*

Here is...	*hic est...*
Look!	*ecce!*

Or	*aut*
Not	*non*
Not at all	*minime*
Sometimes	*aliquando*
But	*sed*
Also	*etiam*
And	*et*, or *que* on the end of a word

FIND YOUR WAY AROUND

Excuse me	*veniam precor*
Where is...?	*ubi ... est?*
How do I get to?	*quis via fert?*
Straight ahead	*directe*
Nearby	*prope*
On the left	*ad laevam*
On the right	*ad dextram*
Is it far?	*longe abest?*
To hire...	*conducere*
...a wagon	*vehiculum*
...a litter	*lectica*

FOOD AND DRINK

Food	*alimentia*
Bakery	*pistrina*
Bread	*panis*
Pastry/cake	*crustum*
Snack bar	*popina*
Fast food	*popina* (same)
Meat	*caro*
Sausage	*tomaculum*
Pie (meat)	*artocreas*
Fish	*piscatus*
Milk	*lac*
Cheese	*caseus*
Eggs	*ova*
Vegetables	*olera*
Lettuce	*lactuca*
Olive	*oliva*
Fruit	*fructus*
Apple	*malum*
Pear	*pirum*
Grapes (bunch of)	*uva*
Fig	*ficus*
Water	*aqua*
Please pass me...	*si tibi placet, da mihi...*
I eat	*edo*
I'm hungry	*esurio*
Is it OK?	*tibi placet?*
It's good!	*mihi placet!*

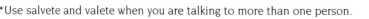

*Use salvete and valete when you are talking to more than one person.

SHOPPING

What do you want?	*quid vis?*
I want...	*volo...*
What else?	*aliquid praeterea?*
Nothing now	*nunc desidero nihil*
That's too expensive	*nimium exigis*
Really?	*etiam?*
Either... or...	*aut... aut...*
Almost	*prope*
Are you open?	*nunc negotium agis?*
I'm only looking	*hodie non emptor sum*
Green	*viridis*
Blue	*caeruleus*
Red	*ruber*
Pink	*puniceus*
Yellow	*flavus*
Brown	*fuscus*
Black	*ater*
White	*albus*
Larger	*major*
Smaller	*minor*
Wider	*latior*
Thinner	*subtilior*
Sandals	*crepidae*
Toga	*toga*
Tunic	*tunica*
Cloak	*pallium*
Buckle/clasp	*fibula*
Brooch	*gemma*
Bag	*saccus*
Leather bag	*follis*
Small bag	*folliculus*
Vase	*vas*
Gift	*bonum*

MONTHS OF THE YEAR

January	*januarius*
February	*februarius*
March	*martius*
April	*aprilis*
May	*maius*
June	*junius*
July	*julius*
August	*augustus*
September	*september**
October	*october**
November	*november**
December	*december**

* In the earliest calendar (adopted from the Greeks and renamed by Romulus), the year probably began in March. This made the current last four months the seventh (*septem*), eighth (*octo*), ninth (*novem*) and tenth (*decem*).

DAYS OF THE WEEK

At the time of your visit, weekdays aren't named. Instead, each month is divided into **Kalends** (1st), **Ides** (13th, or 15th in March, May, July and October) and **Nones** (eight days before Ides.) Days in-between are counted back from these, so 11th May becomes AD V ID. MAI. (AD stands for *ante diem*, or "days before", making it five days before the Ides of May.)

PRONUNCIATION TIPS

For most words you should be understood if you say them as they are written. But bear in mind these three letters:
'c' is pronounced like a 'k'
'v' is pronounced like a 'w'
'j' before a vowel is pronounced like a 'y'

THE VIRTUAL TOURIST

If your trip leaves you longing to return – or you can't get there in the first place – why not take a virtual tour of the Ancient World? Below you'll find descriptions of recommended websites. Before setting out, please read our Internet safety guidelines on pages 198-199.

For links to all the websites on this page, go to the Usborne Quicklinks Website at **www.usborne-quicklinks.com** and enter the keywords "guide to ancient world".

EXPLORING ANCIENT SIGHTS

In **Egypt**, you can:
* explore Tutankhamun's tomb
* fly through a 3-D model of a pyramid
* take a tour of Abu Simbel
* wander around the pyramids, then build a scaled-down model

In **Greece**, why not:
* try the "Acropolis Experience", a 3-D animation of the Parthenon
* discover Athens via an interactive map
* explore Athens, Corinth and Olympia

And when in **Rome**:
* spend a day at the baths, touring the bathhouse of Caracalla
* tour a 14-room villa and see close-ups of ten incredible mosaics

FUN & GAMES

In **Egypt**:
* learn mummification step-by-step

* sail a boat down the Nile in a search for precious stones

In **Greece**:
* play a sliding block puzzle putting smashed pots together
* try a quiz to see who you might have been if you lived in Greece
* take a trip to a play or the Olympics with an animated cartoon

In **Rome**:
* use a do-it-yourself speech maker to write an impressive (or simply silly) speech for a senator
* create mosaic designs
* learn the moves for ball games
* construct an aqueduct
* try out recipes including spicy sausages and boiled eggs in pine nut sauce
* play a life-or-death game where you are emperor of Rome

LANGUAGE LINKS

Egyptian:
* write your name in hieroglyphs
* edit a scribe's manuscript

Greek:
* learn and speak the Ancient Greek alphabet using your keyboard
* use an English-Greek dictionary

Roman:
* write dates Roman style with a speedy date converter

VACATION PICS

No trip is complete without photos to show on your return. Many museum websites have fantastic photos of objects and places and are a good place to start.

GENERAL REFERENCE

MEN & WOMEN AROUND THE NILE

A "Who's Who" of Ancient Egypt is largely made up of pharaohs, since they are by far the most important people in the country. As there are over 300 rulers, however, only a few are listed here. Names in **bold** have their own entry in the list.

Ahmes Nefertari (Dynasty XVIII): sister-wife of **Ahmose** and Queen of Egypt, she ruled on behalf of her son Amenhotep I, until he was old enough to rule in his own right. They founded the community for royal tomb-builders (see page 29).

Ahmose (c.1552-1527BC Dynasty XVIII): the first king of the New Kingdom, he came to the throne as a child. In later years, he freed Egypt from the Hyksos, a people from the east who invaded and occupied Egypt between the Middle and New Kingdoms.

Akhenaten (c.1364-1347BC Dynasty XVIII): the king previously known as **Amenhotep IV**, he elevated the sun god Aten above all others, renaming himself and building a new capital, Akhetaten (modern Amarna). After his death, he was reviled. Egypt reverted to a multi-deity nation, his capital was abandoned and all his monuments were destroyed.

Akhenaten

Amenhotep III (c.1402-1364BC Dynasty XVIII): king of Egypt during a period of peace. Son of Tuthmosis IV and father of **Akhenaten**, who may have been his co-ruler near the end of his reign.

Amenhotep IV (see **Akhenaten**)

Djoser (c.2630-2611BC Dynasty III): king of Egypt, notable for having the first step pyramid at Sakkara.

Hatshepsut (c.1490-1468BC Dynasty XVIII): appointed to rule on behalf of her young nephew, **Tuthmosis III**, she seized power and reigned as "king" for over 20 years. But you won't see much evidence of her reign. Tuthmosis destroyed most of it when he came to power.

A stone carving of **Hatshepsut**

Imhotep (Dynasty III): an official during **Djoser's** reign, he was the architect who designed the first step pyramid. Also a doctor and high priest, he's worshipped as a god in the New Kingdom.

Khufu/Cheops (c.2551-2528BC Dynasty IV): son of Sneferu, his pyramid, the Great Pyramid at Gizah, was the largest ever built.

Menes (c.3100BC): king of Upper Egypt, he conquered Lower Egypt, uniting the two kingdoms to become king of the First Dynasty.

Nefertari (Dynasty XIX): chief queen of **Ramesses II**, one of the temples at Abu Simbel was built for her. She also has a spectacular tomb in the Valley of the Queens.

A painted stone bust of **Nefertiti**

Nefertiti (Dynasty XVIII): queen of Egypt and wife of **Akhenaten**, she was renowned for her beauty.

Pepi II (c.2246-2152BC Dynasty VI): the last king of the Old Kingdom, he reigned for 94 years – the longest recorded reign in history.

Ramesses I (c.1305-1303BC Dynasty XIX): a former army officer and vizier to Horemheb, the last pharaoh of Dynasty XVIII. When Horemheb died without a son, Ramesses took the throne and founded Dynasty XIX. Grandfather of **Ramesses II**.

Ramesses II

Ramesses II (c.1289-1224BC Dynasty XIX): one of the most famous kings in Egyptian history, due in no small part to his gift for self-publicity. He built dozens of forts, temples and monuments, including two massive temples carved into the rock face at Abu Simbel.

In the early part of his reign, he fought the Hittites, who were building an empire in Asia Minor (most of present-day Turkey).

Seti I (c.1303-1289BC Dynasty XIX): **Ramesses I**'s son. Seti began the reconquest of the eastern provinces lost under Akhenaten.

Tutankhamun (c.1347-1337BC Dynasty XVIII): son of **Akhenaten**, he came to the throne when he was about nine and married his half-sister Ankhesenamun. He was so young, a general named Horemheb and a courtier named Ay became regents, ruling on his behalf. Tutankhamun, the "boy-king", was only 20 when he died, but he'll find fame in the 20th century when his tomb is discovered by Howard Carter, an archaeologist.

The head from one of **Tutankhamun's** magnificent coffins

Tuthmosis III (c.1492-1436BC Dynasty XVIII): nephew of **Hatshepsut** and one of Egypt's greatest warriors.

MEN & WOMEN AROUND ATHENS

An at-a-glance guide to the most famous (and infamous) politicians, playwrights, philosophers and scientists in Greece. Bear in mind that some of them lived before your arrival or won't be born until after you've gone.

Aeschylus (c.525-456BC): one of the best-known Greek playwrights, he's written over 80 tragedies. Only seven will survive, so catch one if you can. Credited with being the first writer to bring dialogue and action to the stage, his most famous work is the *Orestia*.

Alcibiades (c.450-404BC): Athenian politician brought up by **Pericles**,* a brilliant but rowdy man and a troublemaker to be avoided at all costs.

Anaxagoras (c.500-c.428BC): friend of Pericles and a philosopher whose theories on the universe will influence many other philosophers.
Not only has he realized that the sun is a ball of flames and the moon merely reflects light, he was the first person to explain a solar eclipse.

Archimedes (c.287-212BC): inventor, mathematician and astronomer, he isn't even born at the time of your visit. But he's worth knowing about, not least because he discovered an important law of physics. Getting into a bathtub, he saw that the water overflowing took up the same space as his body, leading to his excited cry, "Eureka!" ("I've found it!")

Aristeides (c.520-c.467BC): politician and general who is known as "the Just" because he's so good, kind and fair. Particularly remembered for helping to set up the *Delian League*.

Aristophanes (c.445-c.385BC): famous Greek comic playwright and author of over 40 comedies. If tragedy isn't for you, try one of his shows, including *The Wasps*, *The Frogs* and *The Birds*. (Just don't expect animal documentaries.)

Aristotle (384-322BC): the best-known Greek philosopher, he'll study at the Academy, a school to be run by **Plato**. Aristotle won't just simply study science, he'll go on to invent a new one. (Your biology lessons are thanks to him.)

Aspasia (born c.456BC): **Pericles'** partner and mother of his son. Because she isn't from Athens, you'll find plenty of people ready to mock her. But she's beautiful, well-educated and counts **Socrates** as a friend.

Draco (7th century BC): politician who was appointed to improve the legal system and made it harsher. Even laziness became a crime, and one that was punishable by death. **Solon** later abolished most of these "draconian" laws, however, so you can relax and enjoy a lazy break without risk.

Euclid (lived c.300BC): important mathematician who'll write a summary of his predecessors' mathematical ideas. Some of his theories will still be followed in the 21st century.

Euripides (c.485-406BC): author of tragedies, he'll write over 90 plays and win five first prizes at the Athens Play Festival. Famous for his natural style and showing characters' inner feelings, he's been criticized for creating evil characters. But tourists brought up on comic book heroes and villains shouldn't be bothered by them.

* Names in **bold** have their own entry in the list.

Herodotus (c.490-c.425BC): the "father of history", he's the first to establish historical facts and show them as a linked sequence of events.

Hippocrates (c.460-c.370BC): doctor who studies a patient's symptoms, seeking practical causes for illness rather than religious ones. Over 2,000 years later, doctors will still use his promise to treat patients well (the Hippocratic Oath) upon qualifying.

Homer (c.8th century BC): poet who recited epic tales from memory. His works include *The Iliad* and *The Odyssey*, following the Trojan War and what happened afterwards.

Myron (5th century BC): sculptor – look out for his famous statue of a man throwing a discus.

Pericles (c.495-429BC): powerful Athenian politician, who'll be elected war commander for 14 years in a row. He's also the inspiration behind the Parthenon temple in Athens.

Pheidias (c.490-c.432BC): artist who began as a painter and now sculpts. You can see his statues of Athene on the Acropolis and inside the Parthenon. But you'll have to go to Olympus to see his masterpiece: a vast statue of the god Zeus.

Pindar (c.518-c.438BC): the poet laureate of the day, he writes odes to great leaders and sporting heroes.

Plato (427-347BC): brilliant philosopher and pupil of **Socrates**, he'll set up a school called the Academy and write books on how to run an ideal state.

Praxiteles (born c.390BC): Athenian sculptor who will become famous for his statues of the gods, and develop a new and delicate style, in contrast to the grand, formal style of sculptors before him. (He will also carve the first nude female statue.)

Pythagoras (c.580-c.500BC): philosopher and mathematician who lived with a large band of followers who have passed his teachings down the generations. His discoveries on right-angled triangles have proved more lasting than his peculiar ban on meat and beans.

Sappho (born c.612BC): lyrical female poet, who wrote nine books about love, family and friends.

Socrates (469-399BC): philosopher famous for being ugly yet charismatic, his mistake was to point out the government's flaws. Accused of corrupting the young, he was sentenced to death by poison.

Solon (c.640BC-c.558BC): politician who introduced a more humane legal system and encouraged the development of trade and industry.

Sophocles (c.496-c.405BC): prize-winning author of tragedies, who is pioneering the use of stage scenery and is a politician in his spare time.

Thucydides (c.460-c.399BC): politician and historian who's written one of the first history books.

Xenophon (c.428-c.354BC): writer and pupil of **Socrates**, he fought for the Persians and Spartans against Athens and was banished to Sparta.

MEN & WOMEN AROUND ROME

Below are just some of the many notable people in Roman history. (You'll notice it's mostly poets and politicians.) You can check the timeline on pages 196-7 for a more complete list of the main emperors. Names in **bold** have their own entry in the list.

Agrippina (AD15-59): mother of **Nero**, who murdered her husband Claudius, with poisoned mushrooms, so her son could rule. Fed up with her interfering, Nero decided ito have her murdered. After three poison attempts and a collapsing boat failed to do the trick, he had her stabbed to death.

Augustus (31BC-AD14; emperor 27BC-AD14): the name taken by **Octavian**, great-nephew of **Julius Caesar**, when he became the first Roman emperor in 27BC. Augustus took control after years of civil war, bringing peace and prosperity to Rome.

Boudicca (AD?-62): Queen of the Iceni tribe in Britain. Badly treated by the Romans, she led a fierce revolt against Roman rule in AD60 and poisoned herself when it failed.

Caesar, Julius (c.100-44BC): a soldier, politician and writer, who extended Roman territory as far as Britain. In 46BC, he defeated his political opponents and was declared dictator. But some senators feared he would make himself king and, on March 15 44BC, they murdered him.

Cato (234-149BC): a politician and writer whose book *de agri cultura* is the oldest existing work of Latin prose. He also penned *origines*, a history of the Roman people from earliest times.

Catullus (c.84-c.54BC): a poet who wrote love poems and vivid descriptions of Roman life. Catullus was the first to adopt the forms of Greek poetry.

Cicero (106-43BC): a politician, lawyer and writer who was renowned as the best public speaker of his day. Unfortunately, he spoke out against one too many VIPs and was murdered.

Cleopatra (?69-30BC): Queen of Egypt from 51BC to 30BC, she had affairs with both **Julius Caesar** and **Mark Antony**. She supported Mark Antony in his fight against **Octavian**, but when they were defeated in 31BC at the Battle of Actium, she killed herself with a bite from a poisonous snake called an asp.

Domitian (AD51-96; emperor AD81-96): a strong and arrogant ruler who strengthened Rome's frontiers and restored many public buildings. Anyone who opposed him was murdered. He was eventually assassinated.

Hadrian (AD76-138; emperor AD117-138): a scholar and soldier who spent much time with armies in the provinces, building barriers (including Hadrian's Wall in Britain) against invaders. He also built a library in Greece and a palace, Hadrian's Villa, near Rome.

Horace (65-8BC): a poet, famous for his *Odes*, short poems on topics such as food, wine and the countryside.

Josephus (c.AD37-100): a Jewish historian and general, who led a revolt against Roman rule in AD66. Believing "If you can't beat 'em, join 'em", he changed sides when the revolt failed.

Juvenal (c.AD60-c.130): a poet whose *satires* criticized the poverty, immorality and injustices of Roman life.

Livia (58BC-AD29): wife of **Augustus**, she came from one of Rome's most powerful families.

Livy (59BC-AD17): a historian who wrote *ab urbe condita*, a vast history of Rome and its people.

Mark Antony (82-30BC): a soldier and politician who was a consul with **Caesar** in 44BC. After a brief alliance with **Octavian**, war broke out between them. Mark Antony committed suicide after his defeat by Octavian in 30BC.

Marius (157-86BC): a general and politician who won wars in Africa, Spain and Gaul and was a consul seven times. His power struggle with Sulla (a general and politician and originally Marius' lieutenant), was a cause of the civil war which led to the Republic's collapse.

Martial (c.AD40-104): a poet who wrote *epigrams*, short poems about Rome's more lively characters and everyday life.

Nero (AD37-68; emperor AD54-68): an emperor so obsessed with power, he had all those who opposed him killed. He is said to have caused a fire in AD64 which destroyed much of Rome. Finally, he was forced to commit suicide.

Nerva (c.AD30-98; emperor AD96-98): an emperor who treated the Senate with respect, and introduced the system whereby emperors chose and trained their replacements.

Octavian: see **Augustus**

Ovid (43BC-AD18): a poet whose most famous work is *metamorphoses*, fifteen books of poems on myths and legends.

Pliny the Younger (c.AD61-c.113): a writer and lawyer who wrote about his uncle (Pliny the Elder)'s death in Pompeii during the eruption of Vesuvius.

Plutarch (AD46-126): author of *Plutarch's lives*, pairs of biographies comparing Greek and Roman soldiers and statesmen.

Seneca (c.5BC-AD65): a writer, lawyer and philosopher, he was also **Nero**'s tutor and was forced to commit suicide when they fell out.

Suetonius (c.AD69-140): a historian and government official who wrote *lives of the twelve caesars*.

Tacitus (c.AD55-c.116): a historian and consul who wrote the *annals* and the *histories* about the lives of emperors.

Terence (c.195-159BC): a playwright who adapted Greek comedies. Originally a slave, he was freed by his master.

Trajan (c.AD53-117; emperor AD98-117): a superb soldier and general, under whom the empire grew to its largest extent.

Vespasian (AD9-79; emperor AD70-79): the emperor who restored order after **Nero**, and began extensive public building works, including the Colosseum.

Virgil (70-19BC): a poet who spent the last ten years of his life writing his celebrated poem *the aeneid*, the story of the history of Rome in twelve books.

GLOSSARY

A

acropolis: fortified hill top in Ancient Greece

agora: market and meeting place in Ancient Greece

amphora (plural: *amphorae*): large, two-handled jar which holds liquids such as olive oil and wine

amulet: an Egyptian lucky charm

andron: men's dining room in a Greek house

ankh: an Egyptian **amulet** shaped a little like a cross – a symbol of life

An amulet

aqueduct: Roman name for a channel which carries water, often built on a bridge, also known as an aqueduct

arena: central area of a stadium

aristocrat: rich nobleman – the name comes from the Greek word *aristoi* meaning "the best people"

Attica: the state of Athens and the surrounding countryside

B

barbarians: **(1)** anyone not speaking Ancient Greek
(2) anyone living outside the Roman Empire

basilica: a large public building, in or near the **forum**, housing law courts, offices and shops

C

cameo: a miniature carving on a semi-precious stone

cartouche: the oval frame containing a pharaoh's name

Catacombs: a series of tunnels under Rome used as burial vaults

A cartouche

cataract: a place where large rocks block the path of a river such as the Nile

cella: main room in a Greek temple

centurion: an officer in the Roman army

chiton: Greek woman's dress

chorus: actors who speak in unison

circus: a large track in Ancient Rome where chariot races were held

citizen: **(1)** generally: a free man with the right to vote in his own state
(2) in Roman terms: originally, a man born in Rome to Roman parents, who could vote and serve in the army. (By late Republican times, citizenship was being offered to those considered worthy of it and, by Hadrian's time, it was extended to many people across the empire)

A chiton

city state: a city which governs itself and its surrounding territory

consul: Rome's most senior government official. Two consuls are elected annually to run the affairs of the **Senate** and command the armies

corn dole: Roman system of giving free grain to poor citizens

cult: the worship of a particular god or goddess, or following a particular system of religious rites; *see also* **mystery cult**

D

Delian League: alliance made up of Athenians and others, formed to fight the Persians

democracy: political system in

which all citizens have a say in running their state. It comes from the Greek words *demos* (people) and *kratos* (rule)

domus: a private house in Ancient Rome

dowry: money or property brought by a woman to her husband on marriage

Duat: the Underworld, where Egyptians go when they die, ruled over by the god Osiris, king of the dead

dynasty: a succession of rulers, coming from the same family

E

Elysian Fields: the Greek name for heaven

embalming: the drying out of a body to preserve it after death

emperor: supreme ruler of all Roman territories. Augustus became the first emperor in 27BC

Empire: (1) countries conquered and ruled by one state
(2) period from 27BC–476AD when Rome was ruled by emperors

Etruscans: people who lived in northwest Italy and flourished before the Romans came to power. In its early days, Rome was ruled by Etruscan kings

F

faïence: a type of glazed material

forum: an open space in the middle of a Roman town, used for markets, law courts and politics

A faïence hedgehog

fresco: a picture painted on a wall

while the plaster is still damp

G

gladiator: a **slave** or prisoner of war, trained to fight in an **arena**

grammaticus: a Roman teacher

grammatistes: a Greek teacher

gymnasium (plural: *gymnasia*): Greek word for sports ground

gynaeceum: women's quarters in a Greek house

H

Hades: Underworld and the kingdom of the dead; ruled over by Pluto in Greek myths

Hellene: the name the Greeks call themselves

Pluto in his chariot

herm: statue of Hermes guarding a Greek home

hetaira (plural: *hetairai*): woman who entertains men at Greek dinner parties

hieroglyphics: Egyptian writing, using pictures and symbols called hieroglyphs to represent objects and sounds

himation: Greek cloak or shawl

Hittites: people who built up a great empire in Asia Minor and northern Syria in the second millennium BC

hoplite: heavily-armed Greek foot soldier

hypocaust: central heating used in Roman houses – hot air flows through gaps between walls and under floors

hypostyle hall: a hall of columns in an Egyptian temple

I

Immortal: god or goddess

Imperial Rome: the period when Rome was ruled by emperors

insula: an apartment block in Ancient Rome. Each apartment within the block is called a *cenaculum*

Inundation: the annual flooding of the Nile

K

krater: large Greek vase holding wine and water

Kush: a kingdom south of Nubia invaded by the Egyptians during the New Kingdom, then ruled over by an Egyptian viceroy known as the "King's Son of Kush"

L

lyre: a stringed musical instrument

M

ma'at: the balance of the universe according to Egyptian religious belief

mastaba: a brick-built tomb, used for Egyptian royal burials before the pyramids and later by nobles

Medjay: the Egyptian police force, which started out as a peace-keeping force made up of Nubian mercenary soldiers

A member of the Medjay

mosaic: a picture made from lots of small pieces of stone or glass

mummy: an **embalmed** body

N

mystery cult: Greek religious **cult** with secret rites only open to those who had passed certain tests

necropolis: a cemetery

O

obelisk: a tall square column with a pointed top

omen: sign from the gods warning of good or evil in the future

ostracism: vote to banish politicians

ostrakon (plural: *ostraka*): Greek name for broken pottery or stone which can be used to write on

An obelisk

P

papyrus: a reed; also the name for a form of paper made from papyrus reed

patron: someone who supports another person, usually with money or a job

pectoral: an ornament, often decorated with jewels, which is hung on a chain to rest against the chest

Peloponnesian League: alliance of Sparta and others formed to fight Athens

pharaoh: king of Egypt

philosopher: scholar who questions the world around him

R

relief: sculpture on stone panel

republic: a state or country without a king, queen or emperor, whose leaders have been elected by the people. Rome was a republic from the 6th century BC until 27BC

rhapsode: Greek name for a man who recites poetry

S

sacrifice: a gift or offering made to the gods – sometimes fruit, flowers or vegetables; sometimes animals or people

sarcophagus: stone coffin

scribe: someone employed to write and copy texts and keep records

Senate: the group of nobles that governs Rome. By 82BC, there were 600 senators. The Senate's powers are gradually being reduced, as emperors take more power for themselves

shrine: a small temple where a god or goddess is worshipped, or a container for a god's statue

shroud: a piece of cloth used to wrap a dead body

slave: a person with no rights, owned by another. Many slaves in the ancient world are prisoners of war

sphinx: Egyptian statue that represents the sun god; often has the body of a lion and the head of a pharaoh

A soothsayer

soothsayer: a man or woman whom some people think is able to predict the future

sophist: Greek teacher of public speaking

stela (plural: *stelae*): a stone carved with inscriptions

stoa: roofed passageway with columns in Greek architecture

Styx: river to the **Underworld** in Greek and Roman mythology

succession: when a new ruler takes over

symposium: Greek dinner party for men only

T

Tartarus: Greek name for hell

A scene from Tartarus

terracotta: a mix of clay and sand used to make tiles and statues

toga: a long piece of cloth that is draped around the body and worn by Roman **citizens**

tribute: a payment made by one ruler or state to another, to acknowledge the payer's inferiority

trireme: powerful Greek warship with three tiers, or levels, of rowers on each side

U

Underworld: kingdom of the dead (see **Duat** and **Hades**)

V

viaduct: Roman name for a bridge which carries a road across a river or a valley

villa: a large Roman house or estate in the country

vizier: the pharaoh's chief minister

TRAVEL THROUGH THREE TIME ZONES

If you were planning to go straight from one place to another, don't forget: the times are different. Leave Egypt in 1224BC, heading for Rome and you'll be in trouble. The city of Rome isn't founded for another 471 years – in 753BC, if the legends are to be believed. Time charts for each destination are on pages 192-197, but below is an at-a-glance guide to the major events in Egypt, Greece and Rome, side-by-side for comparison.

EGYPT

c.3100BC King Menes unites Upper and Lower Egypt.

c.2649-2150BC Old Kingdom, dynasties III to VI: the pyramids are built.

c.2150-2040BC First Intermediate Period.

c.2040-1640BC Middle Kingdom, dynasties XI-XIV: Nubia is conquered.

c.1640-1552BC Second Intermediate Period, dynasties XV-XVII.

c.1552-1069BC New Kingdom, dynasties XVIII-XX: royal tombs are built in the Valley of the Kings.

c.1450 The Egyptian Empire is at its largest.

c.1289-1224BC Ramesses II is in charge.

c.1069-663BC Third Intermediate Period, dynasties XXI-XXV: a confusing time.

GREECE

c.2900-1250 The Bronze Age.

c.2500BC The city of Troy is built in Asia Minor (modern-day Turkey).

c.1900BC On Crete, the Minoans are building palaces.

c.1600-1200BC The Mycenaeans rise to power in Greece and then, almost as quickly, fall.

c.1050-800BC The Dark Ages (see page 66).

One big question mark

c.800-500BC The Archaic Period.

ROME

Seven Hills

c.2000BC No Rome yet.

. . .

c.1100BC Still no Rome.

. . .

c.900BC The Etruscans establish themselves in northern Italy.

753BC Rome is finally founded; ruled by kings.

EGYPT

During the Third Intermediate Period, several lines of kings rule simultaneously. Egypt begins to decline.

664-332BC Late Period, dynasties XXVI-XXXI. Egypt spends part of the time under Persian rule.

Under Persian rule...

332-323BC The Greek Period. In 323BC, Alexandria becomes Egypt's new capital.

51-30BC Cleopatra VII rules Egypt.

30BC Egypt is conquered by Rome.

GREECE

776BC The first Olympic Games.

c.683BC Magistrates replace kings in Athens.

c.650BC Tyrants rule.

508BC Democracy – of sorts – is introduced.

500-336BC The Classical Era; Greek Art has its Classical Period.

461-429BC Pericles is in charge in Athens.

431-404BC The Peloponnesian Wars.

338BC Philip II of Macedon rules Greece.

336-323BC Philip's son, Alexander, founds an empire.

202-197BC Philip V of Greece is beaten by the Romans.

147-146BC Roman rule is imposed on Greece.

A Roman imposing

ROME

. . .

510 (or 509)BC The Republic is founded.

Kicking the kings out

264BC Rome dominates Italy.

55-54BC Julius Caesar invades Britain.

45BC Julius Caesar becomes dictator.

27BC Augustus is the first emperor: the Empire begins (and continues on page 196).

EGYPT

ARCHAIC PERIOD c.3100-2649BC

c.3100BC Dynasty I Menes unites Upper and Lower Egypt and builds a capital at Memphis. Kings are buried in mud-brick tombs called mastabas.
Dynasty II

OLD KINGDOM c.2649-2150BC

c.2649-2575BC Dynasty III Age of the step pyramids. Architect **Imhotep** builds the first step pyramid, for king **Djoser**.
c.2575-2467BC Dynasty IV
c.2575-2551BC Reign of Sneferu who builds the first straight-sided pyramid.
c.2551-2528BC Reign of **Khufu (Cheops)** during which his Great Pyramid is built at Gizah.
c.2520-2494BC Khafre (Chephren)
c.2490-2472BC Menkaure (Mycerinus)
c.2467-2323BC Dynasty V
c.2323-2150BC Dynasty VI

1ST INTERMEDIATE PERIOD c.2150-2040BC

Dynasties VII & VIII (short reigns of many kings)
c.2134-2040BC Dynasties IX & X A new line of kings rules from Herakleopolis.

MIDDLE KINGDOM c.2040-1640BC

c.2040-1991BC Dynasty XI Egypt is reunified by a prince of Thebes; Thebes becomes the capital.
c.1991-1783BC Dynasty XII A period of great cultural achievement. Nubia is conquered and forts are built.
c.1783-1640BC Dynasty XIII Royal power slowly breaks down.
c.1783-1640BC Dynasty XIV The reign of rebel princes who rule at the same time as Dynasty XIII.
c.1674BC The Nile Delta is overrun with Hyksos, a people from the Middle East.

2ND INTERMEDIATE PERIOD c.1640-1552BC

Dynasties XV & XVI The reign of the Hyksos kings in the north.
c.1640-1552BC Dynasty XVII The reign of Theban kings.

Names in **bold** are referred to on pages 180-181.
The pharaohs shown are those mentioned elsewhere in the guide.

**NEW KINGDOM
c.1552-1069BC**

c.1552-1305BC Dynasty XVIII
c.1552-1527BC Reign of **Ahmose,** conqueror of the Hyksos.
c.1490-1468BC Reign of **Hatshepsut,** a queen who rules as a king.
c.1490-1436BC Reign of **Tuthmosis III,** the greatest of the so-called "warrior pharaohs".
c.1364-1347BC Reign of **Akhenaten.**
c.1347-1337BC Reign of **Tutankhamun,** the "boy-king".
c.1305-1186BC Dynasty XIX
c.1305-1303BC Reign of **Ramesses I.**
c.1289-1224BC Reign of **Ramesses II,** a great warrior and prolific builder, whose rule lasts for nearly 70 years.
c.1186-1069BC Dynasty XX The reign of nine more Ramesses (and a Set-nakht).

**3RD
INTERMEDIATE
PERIOD
c.1069-663BC**

c.1069-945BC Dynasty XXI
c.945-715BC Dynasty XXII
Dynasty XXIII A separate line of kings who rule at the same time as the later kings from Dynasty XXII and Dynasty XXIV.
c.727-715BC Dynasty XXIV Two pharaohs who rule at the same time as Dynasties XXII and XXIII.
c.728-663BC Dynasty XXV The rule of kings from Nubia. Dynasty XXV overlaps with the start of Dynasty XXVI.

**LATE PERIOD
664-332BC**

664BC The Egyptians regain their independence from Nubia.
664-525BC Dynasty XXVI
525-404BC Dynasty XXVII The reign of kings from Persia, including one Cambyses (525-521BC) who lost an army in the Egyptian desert.
404-343BC Dynasties XXVIII - XXX Egyptian princes overthrow the Persians and rule Egypt.
343-342BC The Persians retake Egypt.
341-332BC Dynasty XXXI The second reign of Persian kings.

GREECE

EARLY HISTORY

From **40000BC** Hunter-gatherers in Greece.
c.6500-3000BC People start moving to Crete; potters set up shop in Greece and Crete.
c.5200-2000BC Farming takes off.

THE BRONZE AGE

c.2900BC Population booms in Greece; towns are established; metalworkers set up beside potters.
c.2500BC The city of Troy is built in Asia Minor (modern day Turkey).
c.2000BC The first Greeks to speak the Greek language are identified in Greece.
c.1900BC On Crete, the Minoans are building grand palaces.
c.1600BC The Mycenaeans become top dogs in Greece.
c.1450BC Crete and the Minoans are overrun by Mycenaeans who go from strength to strength.
c.1250BC The city of Mycenae is fortified; the Trojan War (probably) breaks out.
c.1200BC The Mycenaeans lose some power.

THE DARK AGES

By **1100BC** the Mycenaeans lose everything, including knowing how to read and write.
New style of writing introduced in the Archaic Period.
c.850-750BC The poet **Homer** is born, lives and dies around now.

THE ARCHAIC PERIOD

c.800BC The Greeks, especially traders, start getting in contact with the outside world.
776BC The first-ever Olympic Games are held in Olympia (probably).
c.750-550BC The Greeks found colonies around the eastern Mediterranean.
c.740-720BC The Spartans start coming on heavy, conquering the nearby state of Messenia.
c.650BC Tyrants seize power in Greece.
c.630-613BC The Messenians stand up to the Spartans but are knocked back down.
c.621BC Draco comes to power in Athens, laying down draconian laws.
c.594BC The Greeks sigh with relief as **Solon** becomes archon and undoes most of **Draco's** work.
508BC Cleisthenes takes over and introduces democracy – of sorts.
500-494BC Greek colonies in Ionia turn against their Persian rulers.
490BC The Persians are defeated at the Battle of Marathon.
480BC The Persians beat the Greeks at Thermopylae and the Greeks defeat the Persians at Salamis.
479BC The Persians are finally defeated and kicked out of Greece.

Names in **bold** are referred to on pages 182-183.

THE CLASSICAL ERA

c.500-336BC Greek art has its Classical Period.

478BC The Delian League is formed by Athens and allies against the Persians.

461-429BC Pericles is the politician of the moment (for 33 years).

460-457BC The Long Walls go up; the Acropolis is rebuilt after the Persian attack leaves only rubble.

449BC The Delian League agrees a truce with Persia.

445BC 30 Years' Peace is declared between Athens and Sparta.

431-404BC Just over a decade later, the Athenians and Spartans are fighting the Peloponnesian Wars.

430BC A plague hits Athens.

421BC Athens and Sparta agree to keep the peace for 50 years. (Sound familiar?)

420BC Alcibiades becomes leader of Athens.

413BC Athens and Sparta are fighting again.

407-404BC Three successive victories for the Spartans. The Long Walls are knocked down; the Delian League is dissolved; democracy packs up and leaves Athens.

403BC Democracy comes back.

399BC War breaks out between Sparta and Persia. **Socrates** is sentenced to death by poison.

395-387BC Corinth, Athens, Argos and Thebes battle Sparta which is still fighting Persia.

394BC The Spartans lose to the Persians.

394-391BC The Long Walls are rebuilt.

387BC The Spartans lose to everyone else.

338BC Philip II of Macedon conquers Greece. The days of independent city-states are over.

THE HELLENISTIC AGE

336-323BC Philip's son, Alexander, founds an empire which breaks up on his death.

323-322BC The city-states fight for their independence, but don't get it.

323BC on Greek states are ruled by descendants of Alex's generals.

202-197BC Philip V of Greece hands the country over to the Romans – not without a fight, but one he loses.

147-146BC Direct Roman rule is imposed on the whole of Greece.

ROME

EARLY ROME

c.1000BC The Latin people first settle on Palatine Hill.

c.800-400BC The Etruscan civilization takes off in central and northern Italy.

753BC According to legend, Rome is founded. It is ruled by kings for over 200 years.

c.750BC Greeks settle on the southern coasts of Italy and Sicily.

c.600BC The Etruscans take over Rome and rule for the next hundred years.

510 (or 509)BC The last of the Etruscan kings is booted out of Rome, which becomes a Republic.

THE ROMAN REPUBLIC

312BC The Appian Way is begun.

264-146BC Three wars with the Carthaginians in North Africa end in the destruction of Carthage.

214-146BC Wars with, and eventual conquest of, Greece.

73BC Spartacus, a slave, leads 90,000 slaves in a revolt.

59-51BC Conquest of Gaul (France).

55-54BC Julius Caesar invades Britannia (Britain).

49BC Caesar and Pompey (a general backed by the Senate) fight for control of the government.

48BC Pompey is murdered.

45BC Julius Caesar becomes dictator.

44BC Julius Caesar is assassinated. Civil wars follow.

c.33BC Octavian and **Mark Antony** fight for control.

31BC Octavian defeats **Mark Antony** and Cleopatra.

27BC-AD14 Octavian (Augustus) becomes ruler of Rome. The Roman Empire begins.

THE ROMAN EMPIRE

AD43 Conquest of Britain begins.

AD64 Rome burns down. **Nero** blames the Christians.

AD68-69 On **Nero**'s death, power struggles lead to civil war.

AD69 Vespasian's rule: a period of prosperity and military success for Rome.

AD79 The Colosseum opens. Vesuvius erupts. (The two are (probably) not connected.)

AD117 The empire is at its largest, with conquests of Dacia (eastern Europe) and Parthia (Middle East).

AD122 Hadrian's wall is begun.

AD212 Roman citizenship is granted to all free people throughout the empire.

AD235-284 Short reigns of many emperors. Barbarians attack the borders from the north and east. Plagues and famine sweep Europe.

Names in **bold** are referred to on pages 184-185.

AD260-275 Gaul declares independence from Rome.

AD270 Romans abandon parts of the empire, withdrawing from Dacia.

AD271-5 The Aurelian Wall is built around Rome.

AD284 Diocletian splits the empire into East and West for ease of governing.

AD286-296 Britain declares independence from Rome.

AD305-312 Reign of Constantius I, followed by a power struggle.

AD313 Persecution of Christians ends.

AD324-337 The empire is reunited by Constantine, Constantinople is the new capital.

AD337 Constantine is baptized. On his death, the empire is redivided. The eastern half becomes known as the Byzantine Empire.

AD361-363 Julian the Apostate restores the Roman gods.

AD363-364 Jovian restores Christianity.

AD367 Barbarian tribes fleeing the Huns set up their own kingdoms on Roman territory.

AD392-395 Theodosius reunites the Empire.

AD394 Christianity becomes the state religion.

AD402 Goths invade Italy. The Imperial court moves from Rome to Ravenna.

AD410 Rome is sacked by Goths; Britain and Gaul are abandoned.

AD455 Vandals invade Italy from Africa and destroy Rome.

AD476 Romulus Augustus (emperor of the western empire), is deposed by Odoacer, a barbarian. The eastern empire is ruled from Constantinople under the Byzantine emperors.

AD1453 Constantinople is overrun by the Turks.

ROMAN EMPERORS

27BC-AD14	**Augustus**
AD14-37	Tiberius
AD37-41	Caligula
AD41-54	**Claudius**
AD54-68	**Nero**
AD69	Galba; Otho; Vitellius
AD69-79	**Vespasian**
AD79-81	Titus
AD81-96	**Domitian**
AD96-98	**Nerva**
AD98-117	**Trajan**
AD117-138	**Hadrian**
AD138-161	Antoninus Pius
AD161-180	Marcus Aurelius
AD180-192	Commodus
AD193-211	Septimius Severus
AD211-217	Caracalla
AD217-218	Macrinus
AD218-222	Elagabalus
AD222-235	Severus Alexander
AD284-305	Diocletian (East)
AD286-305	Maximinian (West)
AD312-337	Constantine
AD337-361	Constantine's sons
AD361-364	Julian the Apostate; Jovian
AD364-379	Valentinian I; Valens; Gratian; Valentinian II
AD379-392	Theodosius (East)
AD395-423	Honorius

USING THE INTERNET

If you decide to pack a virtual
suitcase, these pages tell you what
you will need. You can also learn
much more about using the
Internet, including any extra
software which may be useful and
– most importantly of all – how to
be safe on your virtual journey.
Remember: you don't just find
bandits in Ancient Greece.

Finally, a reminder: for links to
recommended sites, go to the
Usborne Quicklinks Website at
www.usborne-quicklinks.com
and enter the keywords "guide
to ancient world".

WHAT YOU WILL NEED

The websites can be accessed using
a standard home computer and a
web browser (the software that
enables you to display information
from the Internet). The basic
requirements are:

* A PC with Microsoft® Windows®
98 or a later version, or a Macintosh
computer with System 9.0 or later

* 64Mb RAM

* A web browser such as
Microsoft® Internet Explorer 5, or
Netscape® 6, or later versions

* Connection to the Internet via a
modem (preferably 56kbps) or a
faster digital or cable line

* An account with an Internet
Service Provider (ISP)

* A sound card so you can hear
sound files

SITE AVAILABILITY

The links on the Usborne Quicklinks
Website will be reviewed and
updated regularly. If any sites
become unavailable, we will, if
possible, replace them with
suitable alternatives. Occasionally,
you may get a message saying that
a website is unavailable. This may
well be temporary, so try again a
few hours later or, if it still doesn't
work, the next day.

HELP

For general advice on using the
Internet, go to the Usborne
Quicklinks Website and click on
"Net Help". To find out more about
using your web browser, click on
your browser's Help menu and
choose "Contents and Index". You'll
find a searchable dictionary
containing tips on how to find your
way around the Internet easily.

COMPUTER VIRUSES

A computer virus is a program that
can damage your computer. A virus
can get into your computer when
you download programs from the
Internet, or in an attachment (an
extra file) that arrives with an
email.

We strongly recommend that you
buy anti-virus software to protect
your computer and that you update
the software regularly. You can buy
anti-virus software at computer
stores or download it from the
Internet. To find out more about
viruses, go to Usborne Quicklinks
and click on "Net Help".

INTERNET SAFETY

* Ask your parent's or guardian's permission before you connect to the Internet.

* If you write a message in a website guest book or on a website message board, do not include your email address, real name, address or telephone number.

* If a website asks you to log in or register by typing your name or email address, ask the permission of an adult first.

* If you receive email from someone you don't know, tell an adult and do not reply to the email.

* Never arrange to meet anyone you have talked to on the Internet.

NOTE FOR PARENTS

The suggested websites are regularly checked by Usborne editors and the links in Usborne Quicklinks are updated. However, the content of a website may change at any time and Usborne Publishing is not responsible for the content of any website other than its own.

We recommend that children are supervised while on the Internet, that they do not use Internet chat rooms, and that you use Internet filtering software to block unsuitable material. Please ensure that your children read and follow the safety guidelines above. For more information, go to the Net Help area on the Usborne Quicklinks Website at **www.usborne-quicklinks.com**

EXTRAS

Some websites need additional programs, known as plug-ins, to play sounds, or to show videos, animations or 3-D images. If you go to a site and you do not have the necessary plug-in, a message should come up on the screen.

There is usually a button on the site that you can click on to download the plug-in. Alternatively, go to Usborne Quicklinks and click on "Net Help". There you can find links to download plug-ins. Here is a list of plug-ins that you might need:

* QuickTime – lets you play video clips.

* RealOne Player® – lets you play video clips and sound files.

* Flash™ – lets you play animations.

* Shockwave® – lets you play animations and enjoy interactive sites.

COMPUTER NOT ESSENTIAL

If you don't have use of the Internet, don't worry. This book is a complete, self-contained tourist guide on its own.

Macintosh and QuickTime are trademarks of Apple Computer, Inc., registered in the U.S.A. and other countries.

RealOne Player is a trademark of RealNetworks, Inc., registered in the U.S.A. and other countries.

Flash and Shockwave are trademarks of Macromedia, Inc., registered in the U.S.A. and other countries.

INDEX

Pharaohs, queens, emperors, gods and goddesses are listed in **bold**.
Numbers in **bold** refer to maps.

FURTHER READING

As you travel around, you'll only need this guidebook – and every experienced time tourist packs light. But if you want to read up on the places you'll be visiting before you go, try the following Usborne books:

INTERNET-LINKED ENCYCLOPEDIAS

If you read all of these, you'll know more than the soothsayers...

✶Ancient Egypt
✶Ancient Greece
✶Roman World

POCKET GUIDES

✶Ancient Egypt
✶Ancient Greece
✶Ancient Rome

Or, for an up-to-the minute view of news and events, why not buy a newspaper to read on the journey. Take your pick from:

✶*The Egyptian Echo*
✶*The Greek Gazette*
✶*The Roman Record*

ACKNOWLEDGEMENTS

Boxer, page 88 © Gianni Dagli Orti/CORBIS
Red-figured wine cooler, page 95 © The British Museum/Heritage Images

With thanks to:
Rachel Daynes (extra web research)
Natacha Goransky (timeline design)
Jenny Hall, Museum of London
Nicola Hanna and the Bedford Museum
Ron Sims (photographic references)

This edition first published in 2003 by Usborne Publishing Ltd., Usborne House, 83-85 Saffron Hill, London EC1N 8RT, England. www.usborne.com
Copyright © 2003, 2000, 1999 Usborne Publishing Ltd.
The name Usborne and the devices ♈ 🜨 are Trade Marks of Usborne Publishing Ltd.